Philippians –
Joy in Action

FRANK & SAMUEL GERVASI

MIDWEST CHRISTIAN PUBLISHING

ISBN: 979-8-9985125-0-6

Philippians-Joy in Action Devotional

In Dedication: Written and dedicated to Sarah, Samuel, and Leah Gervasi. The greatest children that God could have ever blessed me with. I am so proud of them for their faith, support of my ministry, and commitment to live out their faith in life. And a special thanks to the co-author Samuel, my right-hand man who is a help to my ministry every day and true pastor in the making....

Library of Congress Control Number: 2025908485

Philippians-Joy in Action Devotional

Introduction:

The church at Philippi was started, during the Apostle Paul's third missionary journey, around 50 or 51 AD. They were definitely not a perfect church but one that was close to his heart.

The Apostle Paul had started it with some of his friends, so he cared deeply about them. The letter itself is known as one of the Prison Epistles. Yet, even under these circumstances he remained joyful and content. Giving us today thousands of years later a blueprint for the right living.

Our hope and prayer are that you faithfully dig in for the next 30-Reflections as we examine, apply, and grow in faith and joy in the:

Philippians-Joy in Action Devotional.

Philippians-Joy in Action Devotional
By Pastor Frank & Samuel Gervasi
Table of Contents

#1 - The Fruit of Thankfulness
Read: *Philippians 1:3-11*

"...so that you may be able to discern what is best and may be pure and blameless for the day of Christ, filled with the fruit of righteousness that comes through Jesus Christ — to the glory and praise of God." **Philippians 1:10-11, NIV**

The popularity and availability of fresh fruit in everyday life has increased dramatically in the last 50 years. This expanded inventory (9,000 items in the 1970s to almost 50,000 items today) means a far more diverse and vibrant range of fruits and vegetables to choose from. However, some take center stage, particularly the banana, America's #1 most-purchased fruit. America's best-loved fruit earned its top spot thanks to the convenience it offers, as well as its versatility. Easy to store in a lunch box or at the bottom of a backpack, the banana is a great snack to enjoy on the go. Bananas are also well known for their high levels of the mood-enhancing chemical tryptophan, making them literally a good fruit. Coming in after bananas at the top, apples, strawberries, and grapes came in 2nd, 3rd, and 4th most purchased (respectively). [1]

Every one of us is growing fruit of some kind – although not the kind you can buy in the supermarket. We all produce spiritual fruit. And as we'll see in our devotion today, a life of thankful joy can have a big impact on the kind of fruit we produce.

Big Idea: A thankful spirit produces spiritual fruit in us that glorifies God.

This church in Philippi – which the Apostle Paul is addressing in these verses – knew Paul well, and vice versa. That's why Paul was so thankful for them and wanted the best for them. Verses 10 & 11 tells us specifically what he desires for this group of believers: *"...so that you may be able to discern what is best and may be pure and blameless for the day of Christ, filled with the fruit of righteousness that comes through Jesus Christ—to the glory and praise of God."* (NIV)

The church at Philippi had already been living out their faith in a way that was noticeable in producing fruit. Paul considered them his *"partners...in the Gospel"* (v. 5) and that they *"shared in God's grace with [him]"* (v. 7).

But Paul also desired them to grow, rooted in this same sense of contagious and invincible joy that he himself had. He specifically desired that: *"...your love may abound more and more in knowledge and depth of insight..."* (v. 9)

Insight: When the church is rooted in Christ and living with thankful and joyful mindsets, God will always get the glory.

Now, some may say that the *"fruit of righteousness"* in our passage is talking about our being made right positionally through salvation, because of the phrase *"through Christ"*. However, it is more likely that he is speaking about the fruit of spiritual growth produced from being grounded in Christ.

Finally, notice the end of verse 11: *"...to the glory and praise God."* The Philippians' life of joyful surrender and obedience to God gave Him the honor He deserved. Let's do the same, choosing to cultivate a mindset of joy, leading to spiritual growth, for the glory and praise of God.

Challenge: Where am I finding my joy? Am I growing in my walk with Jesus?

Pray: Asking God to help me take joy in Him and make my life am offering of worship...

Going Deeper:

What is the significance of the *"fruits of righteousness"* in our passage? In **Matthew Henry's Commentary on the Whole Bible**,

Philippians-Joy in Action Devotional

Henry sheds some light on what these fruits are and how we can acquire them.

"These verses contain the prayers [Paul] put up for them. Paul often let his friends know what it was he begged of God for them, that they might know what to beg for themselves and be directed in their own prayers...He prayed...[t]hat they might be a fruitful useful people... The fruits of righteousness are the evidence and effects of our sanctification, the duties of holiness springing from a renewed heart...Observe [that] Those who do much good should still endeavor to do more. The fruits of righteousness, brought forth for the glory of God and edification of his church, should really fill us, and wholly take us up. Fear not being emptied by bringing forth the fruits of righteousness, for you will be filled with them. These fruits are by Jesus Christ, by his strength and grace, for without him we can do nothing."[2]

Devotion written by Pastor Frank & Samuel Gervasi

---

1. Adapted from *What is the Most Commonly Consumed Fruit in the US?*, as accessed at https://www.buffalomarket.com/blogs/news/ most-commonly-consumed-fruit-in-the-us#:~:text=Bananas.%20America's%20best%2Dloved%20fruit%20earned%20its%20top,con centration%20of%20natural%20fructose%20and%20quick%2Drelease%20energy., on 12/26/2024.

2. *Matthew Henry's Commentary on the Whole Bible*, public domain, as accessed on Bible Gateway Plus, on 12/26/2024.

#2 - A Plan Behind the Cloud
Read: *Philippians 1:12-14*

"...[i]n the same way, the gospel is bearing fruit and growing throughout the whole world—just as it has been doing among you since the day you heard it and truly understood God's grace."
Colossians 1:6b, NIV

Newscaster Paul Harvey tells a story of God's providential care over thousands of allied prisoners during World War II. One of America's B-29 bombers took off from the island of Guam with its eyes set on a target in Kokura, Japan. However, because clouds covered the target area, the aircraft circled for nearly an hour until its fuel supply reached the danger point. The captain and his crew finally decided they had better go after the secondary target. Changing course, they found that the sky was clear, dropped their payload, and headed for home base. Sometime later an officer received some startling information from military intelligence. Just one week before the pilots' mission, the Japanese had transferred one of their largest concentrations of captured Americans to the city of Kokura – the original target of the bomber! Upon reading this, the officer exclaimed, *"Thank God for that protecting cloud! If the city hadn't been hidden from the bomber, it would have been destroyed."*[1]

That thick cloud over Kokura, Japan, was certainly a surprising and unwelcome obstacle to the pilots, but because of it, many lives were saved. We too encounter obstacles and difficulties in life, but as we'll see in our devotion today, God can use those difficulties to give us an opportunity to change lives.

Big Idea: _Our hardships can give us an opportunity to advance the Gospel._

_____

At the time of writing this letter, the Apostle Paul wasn't exactly able to go out into the streets or into people's homes to tell them about Jesus. Paul wrote the book of Philippians from prison.

However, instead of hindering the advancement of the Good News, this development was only working to help, as Paul tells us in v. 12: _"Now I want you to know, brothers and sisters, that what has happened to me has actually served to advance the gospel."_ (NIV)

How exactly was Paul's imprisonment helpful? Well, for one, verse 13 brings up the _"whole palace guard"_ – which probably consisted of a few thousand soldiers. Paul had the opportunity to speak to the guards who watched him about Christ, and he may have already had some experience with them from when he was persecuting the church. Word got around, and soon all the troops knew about Paul's faith in Jesus.

_____

Insight: _Because hardships can lead to sharing the Gospel, we should not be surprised but rather be practical and willing._

_____

In addition, Acts 28:30 (which describes Paul's imprisonment) says that Paul _"...welcomed everyone who came to see him."_ During the time of his imprisonment, Paul was under house arrest. This meant that Paul could not go out, but others could come to him. And Paul used these opportunities to spread the Gospel.

Whatever difficulty we face today, whether it be stress at work, a sickness or ailment, an issue with a bill, or anything else, God could be giving you an opportunity to advance the Good News!

_____

Challenge: What opportunities do I have to advance the Gospel today?

Pray: Asking God to use my life to spread His fame and glory to all around me...

_____

Philippians-Joy in Action Devotional

Going Deeper:

What does it mean that Paul's imprisonment made his fellow believers *"confident in the Lord"* (v. 14)? The **NIV Quest Study Bible Notes** offers its interpretation, and in so doing, gives us an encouragement to be bold as well:

"Courage can be contagious. The world of the early church was not always friendly to the gospel. But even during great hardship, Paul ignored the potential negative consequences and shared the message anyway. His example challenged other believers to be just as bold in proclaiming the gospel." [2]

———————

Devotion written by Pastor Frank & Samuel Gervasi

———————

1. Adapted from a story told by John Nelson Darby, as accessed on https://www.sermonillustrations.com/a-z/g/god_sovereignty.htm, on 1/02/2024.
2. *NIV Quest Study Bible Notes*, Copyright © 1994, 2003, 2011 by Zondervan, as accessed on Bible Gateway Plus, on 1/02/2024.

#3 - Motives Matter
Read: *Philippians 1:15-18*

"But what does it matter? The important thing is that in every way, whether from false motives or true, Christ is preached. And because of this, I rejoice. Yes, and I will continue to rejoice..." **Philippians 1:18, NIV**

"At the village church in Kalonovka, Russia, attendance at Sunday school picked up after the priest started handing out candy to the peasant children. One of the most faithful was a pug-nosed kid who recited his Scriptures with proper piety, pocketed his reward, then fled into the fields to munch on it. But the priest took a liking to the boy and persuaded him to attend church school. By offering other inducements, the priest managed to teach the boy the four Gospels. In fact, he won a special prize for learning all four by heart and reciting them nonstop in church. 60 years down the road, the young boy still likes to recite Scriptures, but in a context that would horrify his old priest. The prize pupil, who memorized so much of the Bible, was Nikita Khrushchev, the former Communist czar. The same Nikita Khrushchev who nimbly mouthed God's Word when a child, later declared God to be nonexistent because his cosmonauts had not seen Him. It seems that the "why" behind memorization is equally important as the "what"; artificial motivation will produce artificial results." 1

The intentions behind why we do the right thing matters to God. And as we'll see in our devotion today, we should have the proper motives when we tell others about Jesus.

Philippians-Joy in Action Devotional

Big Idea: Our motives for sharing the Gospel are important, so we should analyze what our intentions are.

———————————

In our passage, the Apostle Paul lists two contrasting motivations behind why believers in the Philippian church were preaching the Gospel.

Some "...preach[ed] Christ out of envy and rivalry..." (v. 15, NIV) They told others about the Good News because Paul was receiving recognition for his efforts, and they wanted to be better than him – to be competitive.

However, in addition to these selfish evangelists, were a group of people who told others about Jesus "out of goodwill" (v. 15, NIV). The phrase "out of goodwill" carries with it the idea of being rooted in love. These believers shared their faith as an overflow of love toward God for what they had been given in Christ.

———————————

Insight: Our motivation in sharing the Gospel should be not to further our own name or reputation, but the glory of Jesus' name, out of gratitude for all that He's done in our lives.

———————————

Lastly, the Apostle Paul looks at the situation with the Philippian church from another angle. Even though some preached the Gospel with impure motives, the name of Jesus was still going forward rapidly and powerfully, and Paul rejoiced in it!

Verse 18 says, "But what does it matter? The important thing is that in every way, whether from false motives or true, Christ is preached. And because of this, I rejoice. Yes, and I will continue to rejoice..."

Because God is sovereign and in control, He can use even our bad motives to accomplish His purposes. But if we have experienced the goodness and grace of God, how could we continue sharing our faith for the wrong reasons? Our motives matter to God; let's have the proper ones when we share our faith.

———————————

Philippians-Joy in Action Devotional

Challenge: *What intentions do I typically have when I share the Gospel? Am I doing it out of gratitude or other improper motives?*

Pray: *Asking God to help me spread the Gospel with pure intentions and the power of His Holy Spirit...*

Going Deeper:

The NIV Grace and Truth Study Bible notes this about Philippians 1:15-18a:

"Into Paul's encouraging report of Christians emboldened by his captivity to speak the gospel, the apostle inserts a surprising caveat: some preach Christ as Paul's competitors, imagining that their success will frustrate him, making his chains chafe, as it were. Paul describes their motives as envy, rivalry, and selfish ambition, anticipating the caution he will register against self-centered, competitive attitudes that could endanger the Philippians' solidarity with one another (2:1–4). Paul fiercely opposed rival Christian teachers when they distorted the gospel of God's grace into a different message that did not deserve to be called good news (Gal 1:6–9; 5:7–12; 6:12–13) or if their character contradicted Christ's purity (Php 3:18–19; 2Co 11:1–15). Paul readily rejoices in the evangelistic success of his rivals at Rome, so we conclude that, despite their unworthy motives, their message was true to Christ and his grace. Therefore, contrary to their expectation, Paul finds reason to rejoice when their proclamation of Christ yields fruit in changed lives. Thus, Paul sets the pace for Philippians in selfless commitment to Christ's glory, not to one's own reputation. As he does elsewhere, Paul characterizes the gospel as preaching Christ, for the divine Son who became human and his redemptive achievement are the message that brings salvation (Ro 1:2–4; 1Co 1:23–24,30; 2:2–4; Col 1:28)." 2

Devotion written by Pastor Frank & Samuel Gervasi

----

1. Adapted from a story told by Parade Magazine 1962, as accessed on https://www.sermonillustrations.com/a-z/m/motivation.htm, on 1/05/2024.

2. NIV Grace and Truth Study Bible, Copyright © 2021 by Zondervan, all rights reserved, as accessed on Bible Gateway Plus, on 1/05/2024.

Philippians-Joy in Action Devotional

#4 - Eternal Priorities
Read: *Philippians 1:19-24*

"For to me, to live is Christ and to die is gain."
Philippians 1:21, NIV

"In past years there was a football *coach who divorced his wife of 26 years when he left* the college ranks *to become head coach in the National Football League. He said he* needed *a wife while coaching on the college level for social functions, and to show families that he would be looking out for their sons. In pro football,* however, *she was an unnecessary* responsibility *and a distraction to winning. He said winning football was his number one priority and his two sons second;* she simply had to be cut out. *In contrast to this, Tom Landry, former coach of the Dallas Cowboys said, "The thrill of knowing Jesus is the greatest thing that ever happened to me...I think God has put me in a very special place, and He expects me to use it to His glory in everything I do...whether coaching football or talking to the press, I'm always a Christian...Christ is first, family second and football third."*[1]

(Adapted from a story told by an unknown author, as accessed on https://www.sermonillustrations.com/a-z/p/priorities.htm, on 1/09/2024)

These two coaches obviously had very different philosophies when it came to what they prioritized. Likewise, we all must make a choice what is most important to us. And as we'll see in our devotion today, our Heavenly Father deserves to be the first priority in the lives of each of His children.

Big Idea: *Living out our faith and furthering the Gospel should be our highest priority.*

Philippians-Joy in Action Devotional

In our passage, the Apostle Paul recognized that his imprisonment could lead either to his death, or to his release. And yet, Paul had confidence that whichever outcome would come to fruition, Christ would be glorified.

Verses 21 and 22a say, *"For to me, to live is Christ and to die is gain. If I am to go on living in the body, this will mean fruitful labor for me."* (NIV)

Paul knew well that when he died he would immediately experience the culmination of all he had hoped for – being in the physical presence of his Savior. However, if it were God's will for him to remain on earth, it would be for Paul to advance the Gospel. Which implies that if we are believers living on earth, our goal should be to advance the Gospel message in the same way.

Insight: All believers should prioritize sharing the faith and doing God's will as the most important thing in their lives.

Advancing the Gospel doesn't always look like leading someone to salvation or inviting them to church. Sometimes advancing the Gospel takes the form of meeting people's physical needs, or treating others with gentleness and compassion, while still always being *"...prepared to give an answer to everyone who asks you to give the reason for the hope that you have."* (1 Peter 3:15a, NIV)

Charles Spurgeon once said this: *"A Christian...should so shine in their life, that a person could not go a week without knowing the Gospel."*

May we make advancing the Gospel message of Christ a priority in our lives – today and always!

Challenge: What things do I tend to give to greater priority than I should? How important is advancing the Gospel in my priorities?

Pray: Asking God to help me live out my faith for others to see Him through my actions...

Philippians-Joy in Action Devotional

Going Deeper:

How could Paul be so joyful that he didn't even care whether he lived or died? In the **NIV Application Commentary**, Frank Thielman breaks it down for us, and in so doing, gives us an encouragement to lean on God's power and presence to help us see things through such a mind-boggling perspective:

"Paul explains more fully the reason for this remarkable indifference to his physical fate in the second part of the passage…Paul's account of his circumstances prior to verse 21 and his perspective on the future after this verse both demonstrate what his close relationship with Christ means in practical terms. Prior to verse 21, even imprisonment by the unbelieving authorities and ill will from fellow believers could not dampen the joyful character of Paul's life, for God was advancing the gospel of Jesus Christ through these hardships (1:12 - 18a). After verse 21, Paul looks ahead and comments that death is gain, for it will mean the closest possible union with Christ. In the same way, continued life is fruitful labor because it means that Paul will be able both to preach the gospel (1:7) and strengthen the Philippians' faith (1:25). Such a perspective on the hardships of the present and the possibilities of the future **is possible for Paul only because Christ lives within him and gives him strength** (4:13)." [2]

_____

Devotion written by Pastor Frank & Samuel Gervasi

_____

1. Adapted from a story told by an unknown author, as accessed on https://www.sermonillustrations.com/a-z/p/priorities.htm, on 1/09/2024.
2. _NIV Application Commentary_, Copyright © 1995 by Frank Thielman., as accessed on Bible Gateway Plus, on 1/09/2024.

Philippians-Joy in Action Devotional

#5 - A Holy Boldness
Read: *Philippians 1:19-24*

"May I never boast except in the cross of our Lord Jesus Christ, through which the world has been crucified to me, and I to the world."
Galatians 6:14, NIV

Many Christians are afraid to tell others about the gospel for many reasons. Fears abound, images of the various responses of the people will tell, can surface. However, God tells us to share the Gospel message with others around on a regular basis. The *Cambridge Dictionary* defines boldness as this: *"willingness to take risks and act innovatively; confidence or courage."*[1]

However, if one thinks about it, God does not leave us to fend for ourselves when the task is before us. And as we will see in our devotion today, the Cross is where we can get our confidence, and bragging rights really belong to Him.

Big Idea: When Living Out the Gospel-All Boasting Should be in Christ

---

Meaning simply, that whether we are effective in bringing someone to Christ. Or we never see someone embrace the gospel and receive Christ. We are still called to be faithful. Looking at today's passage we see that very thing. And ultimately the result is in God's hand, anyway. Every time we share our faith and, every time we promote the Gospel of Christ. So, don't be discouraged, or feel that you're doing something wrong. The power of the Holy Spirit is what changes people's hearts. Because we read in v. 26: Pause *"Your boasting in Christ Jesus will abound."*

Philippians-Joy in Action Devotional

Now, in this case it was because the Apostle Paul remained, and kind of looks a little prideful, because he says, *"on account of me."* I read that and thought, wow! He's kind of full of himself!

However, I don't think he was boasting but more just acknowledging that the church was not that established and rooted for several years yet. In fact, even though the book of Philippians was written in AD 61 or so. The church at Philippi wasn't established until his second missionary journey. Making the church at Philippi, eight years old or so. Some church plants fall apart well after that time frame.

Consequently, people can impact a churches success or not. But ultimately, if God has ordained for that church or ministry to prosper and move forward it's better that it's in Christ that the boasting and bragging is done.

———————————

Insight: When Living Out the Gospel-All Boasting Should Be in Christ-Because the Gospel's Power is in the Cross

———————————

The apostle Paul understood that the crucifixion was where the power of the Gospel resided. Think about what he says in the epistle of Galatians. In chapter 6, where he was talking about putting confidence in the flesh, and doing those outward rituals to satisfy God in some way. In v. 14 he says, *"May I never boast except in the cross of our Lord Jesus Christ, through which the world has been crucified to me, and I to the world."* Meaning, he only wanted to be known for Christ crucified. Nothing else! Very straightforward!

And nothing else matters or is more important than the gospel message. Either, people accept the message, or they don't. Our job is to be faithful, especially in how we live our lives for others to see.

Greg Laurie says, *"He will not force you to share your faith, but He will prompt you. And when you take that step of faith, He will empower and use you."* 2 Let's be faithful and share our faith today. Boasting in the Cross and leaving the results to God.

———————————

Challenge: Have I been sharing my faith recently? Who can I talk with about the Cross of Christ this week?

Philippians-Joy in Action Devotional

Pray: Asking God to help us boldly proclaim our faith for others to see Him through our lives...

Going Deeper:

The *Zondervan Bible Backgrounds Commentary* talks about the deliverance of Paul when it says,

"Will turn out for my deliverance ... and ... that I will in no way be ashamed (1:19–20).
Although Paul nowhere indicates that he is quoting Scripture when he uses this phrase, it is a word-for-word citation of the Greek version of Job 13:16. Job says that he knows, contrary to his accusers, that his own iniquity is not the cause of his suffering. He uses the metaphor of standing trial before God and says that he is confident that after God has cross-examined him he will be saved. Similarly, Paul knows that whatever the outcome of his trial, when he stands before God he will have no cause for shame but will experience "salvation" (niv, "deliverance"). "[3]

Devotion written by Pastor Frank & Samuel Gervasi

---

1. Cambridge Dictionary, at https://dictionary.cambridge.org/us/dictionary/english/boldness accessed, on 01/12/2024.
2. *Greg Laurie, Tell Someone: You Can Share the Good News,*
https://www.goodreads.com/work/quotes/45656479-tell-someone-you-can-share-the-good-news ,as accessed on 01/12/2024.
3. *Zondervan Bible Backgrounds Commentary,* Zondervan 2002, from www.biblegateway.com, as accessed on 01/12/2025.

Philippians-Joy in Action Devotional

#6 - Worthy Citizens
Read: *Philippians 1:27*

"Therefore, since we are surrounded by such a great cloud of witnesses, let us throw off everything that hinders and the sin that so easily entangles. And let us run with perseverance the race marked out for us..."
Hebrews 12:1, NIV

"*Howard Hendricks* once boarded *an American Airline flight after a very long delay.* One of Hendricks' fellow passengers, *who had too much to drink, was being rude to the other passengers,* and *demanding with the flight attendants.* One of the flight attendants on board tried to calm down the livid traveler and restore order in the plane. *Hendricks watched the flight attendant treat this unpleasant man with class, dignity and professionalism. She was unruffled. Howard was so impressed that he walked to the back of the plane* to praise her for her actions. *He told her how impressed he was* at her response, *and that he was going to write a letter of commendation to American Airlines. In response, she said, 'Thank you sir, but I don't work for American Airlines.' Hendricks was* momentarily confused *until she* clarified, *'I work for Jesus Christ.'*"[1]

This stewardess understood what it meant to let her faith shine through her actions and live with a higher perspective, and others noticed. We too have been called to live in a way that identifies us with Christ, and as we'll see in our devotion today, our understanding of being a citizen of God's kingdom is important if we are to live up to our calling.

Big Idea: *As citizens of heaven, we should live in a way that shows others that we belong to Christ.*

Philippians-Joy in Action Devotional

In our passage today, the Apostle Paul exhorts the Philippians not just to talk about the Gospel, but to live it out.

The first part of verse 27 says, *"Whatever happens, conduct yourselves in a manner worthy of the gospel of Christ. "* (NIV)

More recent translations will often use the phrase *"...live as a citizen of heaven..."* (NLT), which sheds some light on this concept. Any citizen has benefits that come with being a part of that country. For citizens of heaven, some of those benefits include being protected from harm, being given hope through the promises of Scripture, and the ability, in some circumstances, to make choices and choose the road we take.

Insight: All Christians are on display for unbelievers to watch, so we should conduct ourselves in a way that reflects well on who Jesus is, and serves as an example to emulate.

However, as much as citizenship in heaven is bursting with blessings, it also carries expectations. Just as any citizen must be prepared to defend the citizenship, so we must be prepared to defend the faith. Just as every citizen must remain loyal to their country, we must remain loyal to God and not take His blessings for granted. And just as every citizen is expected to handle their freedoms properly, we must use our freedom *"...[not] to indulge the flesh; rather, [to] serve one another humbly in love. "* (Galatians 5:13, NIV)

John Piper once said this: *"God created us for this: to live our lives in a way that makes him look more like the greatness and the beauty and the infinite worth that he really is. "*

Let's be intentional to live out that purpose today, living in a way that shows we deserve to be identified as followers of Christ.

Challenge: *In what areas do I represent Christ in a positive light? In what areas is my conduct representing Him in a negative light?*

Pray: *Asking God to help me live a life worthy of being called a Christian...*

Philippians-Joy in Action Devotional

Going Deeper:

What does living "worthy of the Gospel" entail? The **NIV Biblical Theological Study Bible** expounds the following:

"Paul explains that this worthy living consists in standing united, refusing to be afraid of opponents, and being willing to suffer for the gospel."[2]

Devotion written by Pastor Frank & Samuel Gervasi

1. Adapted from a story told by Ken Weliever, as accessed on
https://thepreachersword.com/2019/09/02/word-of-the-week-work-2/, on 1/16/2025.
2. *NIV Biblical Theological Study Bible,* Copyright © 2019 by Zondervan, as accessed at Bible Gateway Plus, on 01/16/2025.

#7 - An Expected Opposition
Read: *Philippians 1:27b-28*

_____

"Don't be intimidated in any way by your enemies. This will be a sign to them that they are going to be destroyed, but that you are going to be saved, even by God himself." **Philippians 1:28, NIV**

_____

"Sometimes unexpected resistance can stop us.......Isn't that the way it always is when you start doing something you're excited about? Have you ever tackled a DIY project? Perhaps some craft......or home improvement project?......You thought, I can do that! You gathered the supplies, set time aside, and started on the project— but suddenly your work doesn't look like the picture....or.... (think the TV show Nailed It!), and you become discouraged. Or maybe it is harder than you expected, and you begin to think you've made a big mistake......" 1

We too experience opposition regarding our faith. People will sometime avoid us, want to argue, and even minimize our faith in Jesus Christ. As we continue in our study in the book of Philippians this month, the Apostle Paul reminds us of this very fact.

_____

Big Idea: Don't be shocked when others oppose you for your faith.

_____

In our passage today, the Apostle Paul reminds the Philippians to not be shocked when others opposed them for being Christ followers. Implying something very important, that people will oppose us, at times, whether we like it or not. It is a

Philippians-Joy in Action Devotional

matter fact that it will happen at one time or another. So, we shouldn't be alarmed when it does because it's not out of the norm. Look again at v. 28: "Without being frightened in any way by those who oppose you."

Now, it might be helpful to think about this in the context of the language used. Notice what the Apostle Paul didn't say. He didn't say -if you are opposed don't be frightened. He didn't say -just in case you're opposed—don't be frightened. And he didn't mention: -maybe, you'll be opposed. It was given that it was going to happen at that church. Which is also implied that it would happen to us now for the same reasons.

Insight: We should persevere when we face opposition for our faith because believers before us did.

You may remember recently we noted that this was not a long-established church. Or one that was rooted for years and years. They were roughly six to 8 years old. As well as the first and only Christian church in that area, most likely. So they understood perseverance firsthand in what they experienced building that church.

Paul also mentions in v. 27b: "I will know that you are standing together with one spirit and one purpose, fighting together for the faith, which is the Good News." So, if believers before us in the history of the church faced difficulties, we should persevere also. There are many ways that churches are opposed for their faith, both then in the church in Philippi and now. Don't be shocked if it happens to you, for your faith in Christ. Stand strong for Christ.

Charles Spurgeon once said this: "If there is one doctrine, I have preached more than another, it is the doctrine of perseverance of the saints, even to the end." 2

Let's stand strong for Christ when opposition arises from those around us.

Challenge: What opposition have I experienced as a Christian and how did I respond? In what ways can I grow or improve my response and defend my faith?

Philippians-Joy in Action Devotional

Pray: Asking God to help me persevere when opposed by others for my faith in Jesus Christ...

Going Deeper:

Regarding verse 28, the NIV Study Bible expands by saying the following:

"1:28 sign. Persistent opposition to the church and the gospel is a sure sign of eventual destruction, since it involves rejection of the only way of salvation. By the same token, when Christians are persecuted for their faith, this is a sign of the genuineness of their salvation (see 2Th 1:5 and note)." 3

Devotion written by Pastor Frank & Samuel Gervasi

---

1. Adapted from a story told on Illustration Ideas, https://illustrationideas.bible/unexpected-resistance//, as accessed on 1/19/2025.

2. Charles Spurgeon, https://www.princeofpreachers.org/quotes/category/perseverance-of-the-saints, as accessed on 01/19/2025

3. NIV Study Bible, Zondervan Copyright 2011, https://www.biblegateway.com/passage/?search=philippians%201%3A27-28&version=NIV, as accessed on)1/19/2025

Philippians-Joy in Action Devotional

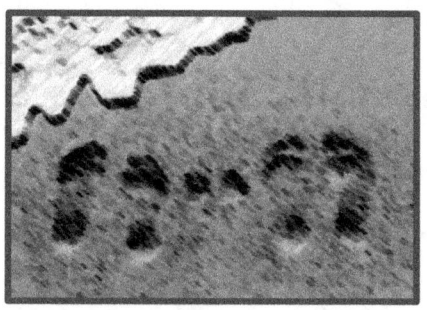

#8 - In the Footsteps of the Faithful
Read: *Philippians 1:28-29*

"Consider it pure joy, my brothers and sisters, whenever you face trials of many kinds, 3 because you know that the testing of your faith produces perseverance." James 1:2-3, NIV

"There is an interesting story about one evening when President Coolidge had company for dinner. He invited some friends from Vermont to join him for a meal at the White House. These visitors were worried about their table manners, so they decided to do everything their host did. All went well until coffee was served. Coolidge poured his into the saucer. The guests did the same. The President added sugar and cream. So did the visitors. Then Coolidge leaned over and placed his saucer on the floor for the cat." 1

Each of us walks in someone's footprints, following someone's example. But what if walking in the footsteps of the heroes of the faith means suffering, loss, and even death? As we'll see as we continue our emphasis on Philippians, sometimes suffering for the faith is inevitable.

Big Idea: When we suffer for knowing Christ, we are following the Biblical example of those before us, so we don't need to be discouraged.

Philippians-Joy in Action Devotional

In our passage today, the Apostle Paul continues his discussion about believers suffering for acknowledging Jesus as the Lord of their lives. He describes suffering in language that makes it sound almost like a gift from God.

Verse 29 says, "For it has been granted to you on behalf of Christ not only to believe in him, but also to suffer for him." (NIV)

Admittedly, this verse is not going to snag people easily into becoming a Christian. I don't think we'll ever hear this as a tag line for any evangelistic campaign. Nevertheless, it is a reality that goes with following Christ.

Insight: People have suffered for their faith over the years, so when you do, have courage that God has called you to walk through it.

The apostles, the very men who walked and talked with Jesus during His earthly ministry, all met brutal and gruesome ends, apart from John. Peter was crucified upside down in Rome. James, Jesus' younger brother, was thrown from the pinnacle of the Temple and beaten to death with a club. Bartholomew was flayed in Armenia. Thomas was run through with a spear in India.

Yet each of these men lived lives that left a lasting impact on the world, a legacy more valuable and distinguished than any secular businessman, politician, or military general. Each of these

men were rescued from death several times before their time to die came. And each of these men

were welcomed into heaven by Jesus Himself, likely greeting them with the words of Matthew 25:21: ""Well done, good and faithful servant! You have been faithful with a few things; I will put you in charge of many things. Come and share your master's happiness!"" (NIV)

Philippians-Joy in Action Devotional

Suffering for Christ is a reality of the faith, that all believers of all ages have experienced. Let's face it with boldness and courage and stand firm on the truth of Christ.

Challenge: In what ways might I suffer for being a Christian? How can I honor God with that situation?

Pray: Thanking God for giving me the privilege to suffer for His name, and asking Him to give me strength and guidance to bear it well...

Going Deeper:

What does the word "suffering" mean biblically? The Encyclopedia of the Bible lists multiple connotations of the word used throughout Scripture, including the kind described by the Apostle Paul in our passage. They define this kind of suffering as testimonial suffering, and say the following regarding it:

"People who choose to live for righteousness in an evil world must expect suffering also from external sources. Service for the Savior runs counter to the aspirations of this world's powers. Followers of Christ may suffer 'for his sake' (Phil 1:29), 'for righteousness' sake' (1 Pet 3:14), 'for the kingdom of God' (2 Thess 1:5), 'for the gospel' (2 Tim 2:9), for resisting Satan (1 Pet 2:19), 'as a Christian' (4:16), and 'for the name' (Acts 5:41)... What response is appropriate when we experience suffering as a testimony to our unhypocritical trust in the Lord? Remembering Christ's example of endurance under stress, we shall follow in His steps (1 Pet 2:21). One should not forget the heroes of faith who 'suffered mocking and scourging, and even chains and imprisonment...' Like Moses, one may consider suffering abuse for Christ greater wealth than the treasures of Egypt (11:26). So believers shall complete the suffering necessary for the building of the Church (Col 1:24), knowing that it assures future glory (1 Pet 4:13)." 2

Devotion written by Pastor Frank & Samuel Gervasi

------

1. Adapted from a story accessed on https://www.sermonillustrations.com/a-z/e/example.htm, on 1/23/2025.

2. Encyclopedia of the Bible, as accessed on Bible Gateway Plus, on 1/23/2025.

#9 - God's Reward
Read: *Philippians 1:27-30*

"Look, I am coming soon! My reward is with me, and I will give to each person according to what they have done." **Revelation 22:12, NIV**

The Our Daily Bread devotion talks about an event, "On December 16, 1944, eighteen members of a reconnaissance platoon held off a battalion of crack German storm troopers in the Belgian hamlet of Lanzerath. Few history books note that their gallant stand gave Allied forces time to begin mounting the defense that eventually won the famous Battle of the Bulge. One of the platoon members was Will James, who after the war slipped into oblivion for nearly 4 decades. During that time he underwent numerous painful surgeries as a result of his wounds in war. Not until 1981, through the efforts of U.S. House Speaker Thomas P. O'Neill and columnist Jack Anderson, was he awarded, posthumously, the Distinguished Service Cross for extraordinary heroism. 1

Most people like receiving rewards for a job well done, or hard work in something. And, when we are speaking about matters of faith, it's the same way. Because we want to be rewarded in some way by God, that we have not done suffered or persevered for nothing. However, God works in His own and time and the way that He feels is best.

Big Idea: The Reward of our faithfulness to live the Christian life will come from God.

Philippians-Joy in Action Devotional

In our passage today, the Apostle Paul continues his discussion about believers and suffering but also that believers will be blessed by God Himself. If you think about it anytime, we do anything for God, there will always be a reward of some kind or another. And in this case, it could be a couple of different possibilities regarding suffering for their faith. However, God was the one who was going to bless the Philippians.

It says in v. 28b: "This is a sign to them that they will be destroyed, but that you will be saved—and that by God." (NIV). The word "salvation" as it is used here is not necessarily speaking about rescued from the kingdom of darkness but may be more in the saving in a general sense. The Interlinear Bible defines the word as: "deliverance, preservation, safety." 2 So, maybe speaking about being rescued from the hardships they were experiencing. Nevertheless, it is also implying that God was the one bringing the reward, even if that meant the blessing was being rescued.

Insight: The reward of God may not be like we think or immediately -however it will come in due season.

We all like receiving gifts and rewards for faithfulness in some areas. However, when it comes to God it may be in a future season. Nevertheless, it will always arrive and in unplanned ways. We sometimes like to dictate how God will bless us, but His ways are beyond us and our ways of thinking.

The reward may also be just experiencing full salvation at a future time, when we will see Him face-to-face. Let us persevere in doing all things for Christ, regardless of what that may be.

Augustine once said, "Our rewards in heaven are a result of God's crowning His own gifts." 3 The reward will come at the right time, and in the correct way.

Challenge: In what ways can I be faithful in the Christian life? What does God have in store for me?

Philippians-Joy in Action Devotional

Pray: Thanking God to bless us in the right season and how He sees fit....

Going Deeper:

What does the idea of sharing our faith bring? The CSB Tony Evans Study Bible lists sharing our faith as the most important honor a believer can have. He says:

"1:28 Courage is crucial to our gospel witness. God, the sovereign King, can embolden failing hearts and eradicate stumbling blocks. Don't be frightened by opponents of the good news....in.... 1:29 Suffering may appear to be a strange gift, but it's not. Suffering for the sake of Christ is purposeful, not purposeless. He allows it for our good and for his glory—and that makes all the difference." 4

Devotion written by Pastor Frank & Samuel Gervasi

---

1. Adapted from a story accessed at: https://www.sermonillustrations.com/a-z/r/rewards.htm, as accessed on)1/26/2025.

2. Interlinear Bible, https://www.biblestudytools.com/interlinear-bible/nas/philippians/passage/?q=philippians%201%3A27-30, as accessed on 1/26/2025.

3. Augustine, Quote Fancy, https://quotefancy.com/quote/905945/Saint-Augustine-Our-rewards-in-heaven-are-a-result-of-God-s-crowning-His-own-gifts, as accessed on 01/26/2025.

4. Tony Evans, CSB Study Bible, Holman, Copyright © 2017 by Holman Bible Publishers, www.biblegateway.com, as accessed on)1/26/2025.

#10 - The Big M-E
Read*: Philippians 2:1-4*

---

*"Because of the privilege and authority God has given me, I give each one of you this warning: Do not think you are better than you really are. Be honest in your evaluation of yourselves, measuring yourselves by the faith God has given us." **Romans 12:3, NIV***

"Harry Ironside was a Canadian preacher and former pastor of Moody Church in Chicago, an accomplished man in ministry to say the least. But despite this, at times, Ironside would become convicted about his lack of humility. So, it was said that a friend recommended as a remedy, that he march through the streets of Chicago wearing a sandwich board, shouting the Scripture verses written on the board for all to hear. Dr. Ironside agreed to this venture and did that very thing – yelling them loudly one after another and making a spectacle of himself. Eventually, he finished his task and returned to his study. He removed the sandwich board, sat down, put his feet up, and thought, "I'll bet there's not another man in town who would have done that." 1

Dr. Ironside wasn't the only one who found it easy to think too highly of himself. Humility is something we all will struggle to maintain at times during our walk with Christ. As we continue in our emphasis on the book of Philippians, we will see in our passage today, how putting others first is intrinsically related to cultivating a humble heart.

Big Idea: Humility means putting the needs and concerns of others higher than our own.

In our passage today, the Apostle Paul links a humble mindset to what we value more: others or ourselves. Verses 3-4 say, "Do nothing out of selfish ambition or vain conceit. Rather, in humility value others above yourselves, not looking to your own interests but each of you to the interests of others." (NIV)

Thinking of others is important when it comes to combating pride. Because pride is naturally self-centered and self-oriented. Pride is all about a two-letter word: M and E – but humility is others-oriented, thinking less of ourselves and more of the people around us.

Insight: One of the main characteristics of someone who is walking in humility is looking out for the interests of others, so we should aim to emulate this quality in our own walk with God!

Oftentimes, people confuse humility with weakness or a lack of self-esteem. But low self-esteem is not the same as biblical humility. A saying I once heard that really captures true humility is this: "True humility is not to think low of oneself but to think rightly of oneself."

Notice the connotation behind the phrase "vain conceit". This phrase comes from a Greek word that means "vain glory, groundless, empty pride". 2

May these words never describe us as ambassadors of Christ! Let's choose to turn away from the hollowness of pride and choose to be humble, let's think more others' needs than our own appearances, and let's allow the Spirit of God to teach us how to think rightly of ourselves.

Challenge: What does it mean to think rightly of myself? How can I focus on others' needs first and foremost today?

Philippians-Joy in Action Devotional

Pray: *Asking God to cultivate in me a humble heart for His glory...*

Going Deeper:

When we fail to value others' needs above our own, our prideful hearts will push too hard to have our own needs (or wants) met and end up destroying relationships and creating rivalry along the way. But humility is the antidote for rivalry. In the ESV Reformation Study Bible, we see this very truth being discussed:

"Pride is competitive by nature and tries to lift a person above others, so promoting conflicts rather than harmony (vv. 2, 14; 1:27). By contrast, humility accepts a place of service, with concern for the needs and interests of others (v. 4). Love (v. 2) is essential for humility (1:9; 1 Cor. 13:4, 5)." 3

Devotion written by Pastor Frank & Samuel Gervasi

---

1. Adapted from a story accessed on https://sermoncentral.com/sermon-illustrations/20206/dr-harry-ironside-a-renowned-preacher-of-the-by-sermon-central, on 1/30/2024.

2. Interlinear Bible, https://www.biblestudytools.com/lexicons/greek/kjv/kenodoxia.html, as accessed on 1/30/2025.

4. ESV Reformation Study Bible, Copyright © 2015 by P & R Publishing, generously provided by Ligonier Ministries, www.biblegateway.com, as accessed on 1/30/2025.

#11 - Serving Models Christ
Read: *Philippians 2:5-8*

"Now that I, your Lord and Teacher, have washed your feet, you also should wash one another's feet. I have set you an example that you should do as I have done for you." John 13:14-15 NIV

A story was told about D.L Moody and exercising humility through service. It was said: "A large group of European pastors came to one of D. L. Moody's Northfield Bible Conferences in Massachusetts in the late 1800s. Following the European custom of the time, each guest put his shoes outside his room to be cleaned by the hall servants overnight. But of course, this was America and there were no hall servants.

Walking the dormitory halls that night, Moody saw the shoes and determined not to embarrass his brothers. He mentioned the need to some ministerial students who were there but met with only silence or pious excuses. Moody returned to the dorm, gathered up the shoes, and, alone in his room, the world-famous evangelist began to clean and polish the shoes. Only the unexpected arrival of a friend amid the work revealed the secret.

When the foreign visitors opened their doors the next morning, their shoes were shining. They never knew by whom. Moody told no one, but his friend told a few people, and during the rest of the conference, different men volunteered to shine the shoes in secret.1

Humility is shown through service to others around us. Just like in the story of D.L. Moody, we also show humility when we humble ourselves and serve others. As we continue in our emphasis in the book of Philippians, we see that Christ was the greatest servant of all, leaving an example for us today.

Big Idea: A Humble Person Will Model Christ by Serving Others...

In our passage today, the Apostle Paul links a humble mindset to modeling Christ's behavior. Modeling was probably the most significant way that Christ taught during his earthly ministry. Verse 5 says, "have the same mindset as Christ Jesus had." (NIV). During his three years of ministry, he did that very thing with his own disciples. In fact, they did everything together. They ate together, lived together, worshiped together, even travelled and ministered together also.

However, by implication they also served each other as well. Because also in verse 5, the apostle Paul noted: "In your relationships with each with one another." So, it was in essence telling them to serve those around them, and they were around each other the most. In addition to the various people, they encountered.

Insight: One of the main characteristics of someone who is walking in humility is serving others. Jesus did and so should we....

It was noted in Thursday's devotion that: oftentimes, people confuse humility with weakness. And humility is not only thinking right of oneself but also shown through service to others. However, because Christ modelled it servanthood to his disciples, we should also serve those around us today.

The highlighted verse from John chapter 13 shows humility in service as well. In fact, if Jesus the Son of God was not too prideful to serve his own disciples, it should serve as our best example to do the same. In John 13:14-15 it shows: "Now that I, your Lord and Teacher, have washed your feet, you also should wash one another's feet. I have set you an example that you should do as I have done for you."

Think about how he got up from the table, putting on an outer garment and stooping down to do something as simple as washing a person's feet, and how it speaks at such volume. In fact, Peter is beside himself and wants no part of it. In John 13 he says: "He came to Simon Peter, who said to him, 'Lord, are you going to wash my feet?'.....'No,' said Peter, 'you shall never wash my feet.'" (NIV, vv. 6, 8).

Humility will always be shown through service to others. My we follow our Lord's example and serve those around us.

Challenge: Have I walked in humility lately? Who can I serve to model Christ's humility today?

Pray: Asking God to cultivate in me a humble heart for His glory by serving others...

Going Deeper:

When we model Christ's behavior it becomes clear to see he was a true servant in every sense of the word. Even though he was the Son of God and God in human form, serving was not beneath him. In the Zondervan Illustrated Bible Backgrounds Commentary of the New Testament, we see this very truth being shown:

"Taking the very nature of a servant (2:7). The word translated "servant" in the niv is the common word for "slave" (see comments on 1:1). But in what sense did Jesus take the form of a slave? From the standpoint of the Romans, Jesus was a common Jew, a member of a people whom the Roman general Pompey had conquered in 63 b.c. and over whom the Romans had ruled ever since, sometimes directly through governors and sometimes indirectly through puppet kings such as Herod the Great, his son Archelaeus, and his grandson Herod Agrippa I. From the Jewish perspective, however, rule by a foreign power was slavery—well-deserved punishment for breaking God's law (Deut. 28:68; Ezra 9:9). Jesus became just such a slave, sharing the curse of the law that had fallen on God's people (Gal. 3:10; 4:4), although he alone among God's people had broken none of God's laws." 2

Devotion written by Pastor Frank & Samuel Gervasi

---

1. Adapted from a story accessed on https://bible.org/illustration/man-servant%E2%80%99s-heart, on 02/02/2024.

2. Zondervan Illustrated Bible Backgrounds Commentary of the New Testament, Copyright 2002, BibleGateway Plus, https://www.biblegateway.com/passage/?search=Philippians%202%3A5-8&version=NIV, as accessed on 02/02/2025.

#12 - Humility Is a Choice
Read: *Philippians 2:5-8*

"And being found in appearance as a man, he humbled himself by becoming obedient to death – even death on a cross!" ***Philippians 2:8 NIV***

"There was a U.S. soldier by the name of William Edward Adams who was posthumously awarded the Medal of Honor. Stationed in the province of Kontum during the Vietnam War, Major Adams distinguished himself on May 25, 1971, while serving as a helicopter pilot. On that date...Adams volunteered to fly a lightly armed helicopter... to a small fire base under attack by a large enemy force...to evacuate three seriously wounded soldiers. There were numerous antiaircraft weapons around the base that the enemy had overrun, but Adams volunteered to rescue his comrades anyway. As he approached the base, the enemy gunners opened fire with heavy machine guns. Undaunted by the fusillade, he continued his approach, landed the aircraft at the fire base, and patiently waited until the wounded soldiers were placed on board. As Adams' helicopter took off to return to home base, it was struck and seriously damaged by the enemy. Adams attempted a safe crash landing, but despite his valiant efforts, the helicopter exploded, and Adams and the wounded soldiers he came to save lost their lives." [1]

William Adams knew before he got into his helicopter that the odds were stacked against him, and the chances of returning successfully weren't in his favor. But he chose to fly in anyway. He made a conscious decision to humbly lay his own life on the line for the well-being of others. There is Another who also laid His life on the line, not to save us from bombs and bullets, but from the penalty of our sin. And as we'll see in our passage today, Jesus' decision to go the cross serves as an example to us, that we too must decide to be humble.

Big Idea: In the same way Christ chose to give His life for us, we must make a conscious choice to humbly put others first.

In our passage today, the Apostle Paul gives us an example of what true humility looks like. Notice how he says in verses 7-8: "Rather, he made himself nothing by taking the very nature of a servant, being made in human likeness. And being found in appearance as a man, he humbled himself by becoming obedient to death – even death on a cross!" (NIV)

Notice how Paul uses the word "humbled" as a verb – implying action! We must choose to show

humility. This idea is reiterated in verse 7 when he says Christ "made himself" nothing, again implying a conscious resolve to do so by His own free will. Humility is not something that comes naturally to us; we must actively cultivate a humble heart!

Insight: Because Christ gave up the glories of heaven to save our souls, we should lay down our pride and serve others humbly in love.

Notice the exclamation at the end of verse 8: "...even death on a cross!" (NIV) Death by crucifixion was usually reserved for criminals, so it was a shameful, and humbling, way to die. But Christ made that choice to give up His divine privileges to redeem us!

And in spite of all of Major William Adams' bravery in Vietnam, because of his human limitations, he was unable to save those he came for. But through the limitless power of God, Christ successfully purchased us through the cross and rescued those He came to die for. And we are called, as His children, to display the same selfless humility toward others.

F.B. Meyers, a friend of D.L. Moody and evangelist in England, once said this: "I used to think that God's gifts were on shelves one above another, and the taller we grow, the easier we can reach them. Now I find that God's gifts are on shelves one beneath another, and the lower we stoop, the more we get." 2 (emphasis added)

Challenge: *How can I keep myself from becoming prideful today? How can I humbly serve those around me?*

Pray: *Thanking God for saving me, and asking Him to help me grow in humble service...*

Going Deeper:

Just how much humility did it take for Jesus to die for our sins? In the ESV Global Study Bible, we see the extent of Christ's humility in the following excerpt:

"It is remarkable enough that God the Son would take on human form for a broken world. But Jesus went much farther, becoming obedient (compare Rom. 5:19) to the point of death, even death on a cross. Crucifixion was the ultimate humiliation, and the physical pain was terrible (see note on Matt. 27:35). It was the total opposite of the divine majesty of the preexistent Christ. Thus, it was the ultimate expression of Christ's obedience to the Father." 3

Devotion written by Pastor Frank & Samuel Gervasi

---

1. Adapted from a story accessed on https://www.cmohs.org/recipients/william-e-adams, on 2/06/2024.

2. Quote by F.B. Meyer, adapted by Andrew Murray in Humility: The Journey Towards Holiness. https://www.goodreads.com/quotes/7272326-i-used-to-think-that-god-s-gifts-were-on-shelves-one.

3. ESV Global Study Bible, Copyright © 2012 by Crossway. All rights reserved. As accessed at BibleGateway Plus, https://www.biblegateway.com/passage/?search=philippians%202%3A5-8&version=NIV, on 02/06/2025.

Philippians-Joy in Action Devotional

#13 - Humility Is Rewarded
Read: *Philippians 2:9-11*

"But he gives us more grace. That is why Scripture says: 'God opposes the proud but shows favor to the humble.'" **James 4:6 NIV**

I once heard a story about Edward Stanton who, "was a lawyer and politician who served as Abraham Lincoln's secretary of war during the American Civil War. Stanton was a close ally of Lincoln and played a key role in the Union's war effort." 1 However, rumors had circulated that during the war Lincoln made a choice by issuing a command that affected Stanton. Consequently, Lincoln's trusted friend didn't immediately follow the order. In fact, Stanton was said to call him a fool! However, when Lincoln heard of what he was called, his reply was "then I must be acting like one." And, after the two talked, he heard the logic, and in humility, and rescinded the order. 2.

Big Idea: A Humble Person is rewarded by God Himself.

In our passage today, the Apostle Paul gives us an important reason for a person to show humility like Christ, that God Himself rewards it. Now, if we think about that, we see that God, himself will work on behalf of the person who is making the conscious choice of lowering themselves by walking and operating in a humble spirit. In fact, we get to experience the joy and peace that comes with that choice.

Notice what he says in verse 9, "Therefore, God elevated Him to the place of highest honor." The elevating was done by someone greater. In this case God did because of the act of submission. Which by implication, is that God will do the same for those who choose this trait in their own lives.

Now, for clarification, obviously it's a different place of honor because this was speaking of the Second Person of the Trinity. Doing what was required to reconcile man back to God and restore all that was destroyed by the Fall of Man. However, I believe, God desires to reward those who walk in humility as well.

Insight: We Should Strive for Humility Not Only Because It's Rewarded, but Also, to Avoid God's Opposition.

Meaning, that God Himself will actively work against the person who is walking in pride. In fact, if we look again at our highlighted verse in James chapter 4, we can see it. Because it says: "But he gives us more grace. That is why Scripture says: 'God opposes the proud but shows favor to the humble.'"

Who wouldn't want to experience the grace of God in greater measure? And conversely, who would want to have God oppose them? It would be a battle that everyone would lose.

May we choose humility and experience the blessings of God's grace in our lives today!

Challenge: How can I keep myself from becoming prideful today? What practical ways can I walk in humility?

Pray: Asking God for more of His grace in our lives by choosing to avoid prideful living.

Going Deeper:

What was Christ exulted to? In the Zondervan Illustrated Bible, we see the response of God the Father because of the humility exhibited by Christ.

Philippians-Joy in Action Devotional

"Exaltation of Christ. The term covers the sequence of events that begins with the Resurrection of Christ and that includes his Ascension and his coming again (see Eschatology). The outcome of his humility and obedience, the "high exaltation" of Christ, will in turn lead to the bowing of every knee and the acknowledgment of his Lordship by every tongue (Phil. 2:8-11; cf. Acts 2:33). The exaltation of Christ places him "at the right hand of God" (Rom. 8:34), an expression used by Stephen (Acts 7:55-56), Paul (Eph. 1:20), Peter (1 Pet. 3:22), and the writer to the Hebrews (Heb. 1:3; 10:12; 12:2). This firmly establishes the association of Christ with God in power and glory, a glorification noted by our Lord himself (Jn. 17:5; cf. 12:32)." 3

Devotion written by Pastor Frank & Samuel Gervasi

1.Wikipedia,https://www.google.com/search?q=abraham+lincoln+and+edward+stanton&oq=abraham+lincoln+and+edward+stanton&gs_lcrp=EgZjaHJvbWUyBggAEEUYOTINCAEQABiGAxiABBiKBTINCAIQABiGAxiABBiKBTINCAMQABiGAxiABBiKBTINCAMQABiGAxiABBiKBTIKCAQQABiABBiiBDIKCAUQABiABBiiBDIKCAYQABiiBBiJBdIBCTE2NTUwajBqNKgCALACAQ&sourceid=chrome&ie=UTF-8, on 2/06/2024.

2. Adapted by a story on, https://sermoncentral.com/sermon-illustrations/67817/abraham-lincoln-s-secretary-of-war-edwin-by-ajai-prakash, as accessed on 02/08/2025.

3. Bible Gateway Plus, https://www.biblegateway.com/passage/?search=Philippians%202%3A9-11&version=NIV, as accessed on 02/08/2025.

#14 - Obedience is Hard Work
Read: *Philippians 2:12-13*

"Do your best to present yourself to God as one approved, a worker who does not need to be ashamed and who correctly handles the word of truth."
2 Timothy 2:15, NIV

"In May 2013, thirteen-year-old Arvind Mahankali correctly spelled the word kneidel (a German-Yiddish word for a dumpling) to win the 86th Scripps National Spelling Bee. Mahankali had finished third each of the two previous years, during which he was eliminated for failing to correctly spell a German-derived word. So, in preparation for his third attempt at the prize, Mahankali diligently worked to strengthen his area of weakness. 'This year I prepared German words, and I studied them, so when I got German words this year, I wasn't worried,' he said after his victory. No one has yet invented a way of acquiring...anything worthwhile—without effort." 1

Sometimes, in our walk with Christ, there will come times when we need to work hard to strive for spiritual growth. We were called to train ourselves to live godly lives, even when it doesn't come easily. And as we'll see in our passage today, this kind of hard work is crucial if we are to live a life that glorifies God appropriately.

Big Idea: We should press hard into matters of the faith, to do our best and live a life that honors God.

In our passage today, the Apostle Paul challenges the believers to continue being obedient, even though he is not present with those believers. He says it's important, in verse 12, that they, "Work hard to show the results of your salvation, obeying God with deep reverence and fear." (NLT)

Every season of a believer's life should be one of deliberately working and applying the truths of Scripture to our own experiences, to live out our faith.

Insight: Christ-followers should press hard into the Christian faith to worship God through their obedient actions.

Verse 12 says to work hard "with deep reverence and fear" (NLT). Some versions translate this phrase, "with fear and trembling" (NIV). This second phrasing has led some to interpret these verses to say new believers should not be overly confident in their faith. But the phrase "with deep reverence and fear" sheds a different light on this verse. We work hard not out of fear or uncertainty whether our faith is genuine, but

from a place of awe and amazement at the mercy God has shown to us.

Finally, it's important to note that Paul's exhortation to work hard in our faith is not suggesting we try to do right by our own power, or by following rules. That would contradict the Gospel, and our passage itself says, "For God is working in you, giving you the desire and the power to do what pleases him."

But just because God is working in us to become more like Him, does not change the fact that we must train ourselves spiritually. In fact, it demonstrates faith that God will help us grow when we discipline ourselves to do right.

We must press hard into the things of God, going all in on living like Jesus. And with the power of the Holy Spirit working in us, we can live a life that Jesus wants.

Challenge: What are the motivations behind why I do the right thing? In what area can I discipline myself to be godly today?

Pray: Asking God to give me the desire and the strength to do what pleases Him...

Philippians-Joy in Action Devotional

Going Deeper:

What does it mean that God works in us? In the 2nd edition of his NKJV Study Bible, John MacArthur elaborates on this phrase:

"Although the believer is responsible to work (v. 12), the Lord actually produces the good works and spiritual fruit in the lives of believers (John 15:5; 1 Cor. 12:6). This is accomplished because He works through us by His indwelling Spirit (Acts 1:8; 1 Cor. 3:16, 17; 6:19, 20; cf. Gal. 3:3)...God energizes both the believer's desires and his actions. The Gr. word for 'will' indicates that He is not focusing on mere desires or whimsical emotions, but on the studied intent to fulfill a planned purpose. God's power makes His church willing to live godly lives (cf. Ps. 110:3)." 2

Devotion written by Pastor Frank & Samuel Gervasi

---

1. Adapted from a story accessed at https://ministry127.com/resources/illustration/the-necessity-of-preparation, on 2/13/2024.

2. NKJV MacArthur Study Bible, 2nd Edition, Copyright © 1997, 2006, 2019 by Thomas Nelson. All rights reserved. As accessed at Bible Gateway Plus, https://www.biblegateway.com/passage/?search=philippians%202%3A12-13&version=NIV, on 02/13/2025.

Philippians-Joy in Action Devotional

#15 - Living Right is Crucial
Read: *Philippians 2:14-15*

"Live clean and innocent lives as children of God." **Philippians 2:15 NIV**

"I read about an instant cake mix that was a big flop. The instructions said all you had to do was add water and bake. The company couldn't understand why it didn't sell -- until their research discovered that the buying public felt uneasy about a mix that required only water. Apparently, people thought it was too easy. So the company altered the formula and changed the directions to call for adding an egg to the mix in addition to the water. The idea worked and sales jumped dramatically." 1

It reminds me of our walk with Christ; we are called to live in ways that honor God. Unfortunately, we mix other things in with God's commands but all he is requiring that is that we live in ways without grumbling and complaining. Especially since people are constantly watching us because we claim to be Christ-followers.

Big Idea: Continuing in Joy Will Speak Volumes to Those Around Us.

As we continue on in our emphasis in Philippians, we see that when we continue in Joy, that it speaks volumes to others. So, if we like it or not, people are watching us both believers but also non-believers. So, because of that we should strive to be living in ways that brings God honor.

Philippians-Joy in Action Devotional

In our passage today, we can see in verse 14 that it says: "Do everything without grumbling and complaining." Now, that's a convicting thing to do if you think about it, depending on the situation. Many things can happen in life that rob our joy. Consequently, it's important that a believer is conscious and doesn't become discontented or complain. For other believers its important because it models how God wants us to behave in the World. Additionally, we should live without grumbling because non-believers will see it.

Insight: Christ-followers should live in a joyous way, so others don't criticize us and cast a bad light on Christianity.

Unfortunately, people will sometimes try and find fault with how a Christian lives and will use that as the excuse to not embrace the things of God. In verse 15 it says: "So that no one can criticize you." We should not give people a reason to accuse us of wrongdoing.

The Apostle Paul even goes further and gives us additional ways to live right. Because in the second part of verse 15 he says: "Live clean and innocent lives as children of God." Clean as used here is the idea of blameless but not perfect. Crooked as some versions use carries the idea of wicked. And, perverse is similar but really means wicked.

A.W. Tozer said it like this concerning right living: "One of the most stinging criticisms made against Christians is that their minds are narrow and their hearts are small....that such a charge can be made at all is sufficient cause for serious heart searching and prayer." 2

May we be people who live right before God, in joy, because others are watching our lives!

Challenge: What does my life look like to those around me? In what ways do I need to grow and become more Christlike?

Pray: Asking God to give us the strength to live in upright ways....

Going Deeper:

What does it mean to live in the right ways? Sometimes it's easy to confuse the word blameless with perfection. However, it's not necessarily the same thing. In the NIV Study Bible, it elaborates on this question and idea:

"Blameless and pure . . . without fault. Not absolute, sinless perfection, but wholehearted, unmixed devotion to doing God's will (see 1:10 and note). warped and crooked generation. A description of the unbelieving world (see Ac 2:40; Eph 2:1–3; cf. Mt 17:17). shine among them like stars. The contrast, like light in darkness, that Christians are to be to the world around them (cf. Mt 5:15–16) .3

———————————

Devotion written by Pastor Frank & Samuel Gervasi

———————————

1. Sermon Illustrations, https://www.sermonillustrations.com/a-z/w/works_righteousness.htm, as accessed on 2/16/2025.

2. Sermon titled: Shining Like Bright Lights for Christ, PFG, Original source unknown.

3. NIV Study Bible, Copyright © 1985, 1995, 2002, 2008, 2011 by Zondervan, accessed in Bible Study Tools on 02/16/2025.

#16 - A Life Well Lived
Read: *Philippians 2:16-18*

"Therefore, my dear brothers and sisters, stand firm. Let nothing move you. Always give yourselves fully to the work of the Lord, because you know that your labor in the Lord is not in vain." **1 Corinthians 15:58 NIV**

"'GO FOR SOULS and go for the worst!' was the constant cry of William Booth, founder of the Salvation Army. The multitudes in London's slums...drunkards, morphine addicts, prostitutes, and the poor...living in abject poverty, convinced him he had discovered his life's work and no one ever took the Gospel to the "down and outer" like he did...He set out to reach them with what he called the 3 S's: soup, soap and salvation...In 1865, Booth started with only his wife at his side...unappreciated by the established churches of his day, ridiculed and jeered by most everyone. His death 47 years later sharply contrasted as 40,000 attended his funeral service, including Queen Mary of England. His "Army" including 21,203 officers and 8,972 societies were working in 58 countries preaching the Gospel in 34 languages!" 1

Hearing about the success stories of men like William Booth excites us, because most of us strive to live faithful lives before God and others. Fortunately for us, faithfulness to God always pays off, and as we'll see in our devotion today our faithfulness will be succeeded by a spirit of joy in the end.

Big Idea: A life of faithfulness will result in joy for everyone involved.

Philippians-Joy in Action Devotional

In our passage today, the Apostle Paul instructs the Philippian believers to be steadfast in their faith. But he also recognizes that, even if he is not on earth to see their faith lived out, Paul still possesses joy. He says in verse 17, "But I will rejoice even if I lose my life, pouring it out like a liquid offering..." (NLT)

A person who is walking faithfully is promised that they will get to experience the joy and satisfaction of a job well done, and a life well lived.

Insight: A devoted heart that seeks to do God's will, will lead to overflowing joy in the end.

Notice how Paul acknowledges the possibility of him "losing his life" in verse 17. The Apostle Paul was willing to even suffer death for his faith. And one of the things that brought him joy in the face of that was seeing the Philippian church grow and serve together for the advancement of the Gospel.

Part of the reason we so enjoy hearing stories of people like William Booth, or even the Apostle Paul, is because the spiritual impact they left behind was large and noticeable for all to see. But make no mistake: all faithfulness to God will be rewarded and can lead to joy in our lives if we let it. Let's welcome that joy today, and keep being faithful, for, "...at the proper time we will reap a harvest if we do not give up." (Galatians 6:9, NIV)

Challenge: In what areas is God calling me to be faithful? How can I experience the joy of a life well lived today?

Pray: Thanking God for the rewards He has in store for me, and asking Him to help me remain faithful today...

Going Deeper:

Paul mentions in verse 17 being poured out like a "liquid offering" or "drink offering". But what does this phrase mean, and what is its significance? The authors of the Dictionary of Bible Themes define it as follows, and in so doing, reveal Paul's belief that laying down His life for the Gospel was an act of worship to God:

"A sacrificial offering of wine poured out at the foot of the altar, to accompany a burnt, fellowship or grain offering." 2

_____

Devotion written by Pastor Frank & Samuel Gervasi

_____

1. Adapted from two stories, accessed at https://www.gospeltruth.net/booth/boothbioshort.htm, and https://ministry127.com/resources/illustration/serving-god-with-or-without-vision, on 2/21/2024.

2. Dictionary of Bible Themes, Scripture index copyright Martin H. Manser, 2009. As Editor, Martin Manser wishes to thank all those who compiled or edited the NIV Thematic Study Bible, on which this work is based. Dictionary accessed at Bible Gateway Plus, https://www.biblegateway.com/passage/?search=philippians%202%3A16-18&version=NIV, on 2/21/2025.

3. Music Intro/Outro, Praise Adonai, Integrity Music, Paul Biloche, 2009

Philippians-Joy in Action Devotional

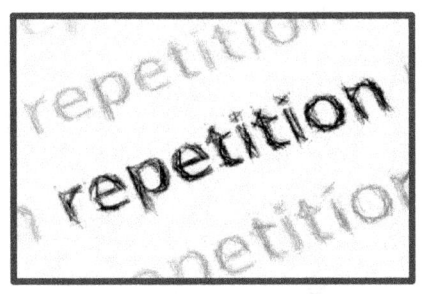

#17 - Positive Repetition
Read: *Philippians 3:1-2*

"These commands that I give you today are to be on your hearts."
Deuteronomy 6:6, NIV

People and athletic enthusiasts have known about the importance of repetition for a long time. One enthusiast said that repetition is what causes muscle to grow by the actual doing of the exercise again and again. He went on to say: "Muscle memory is the idea in sports where you, to truly master something, you must do it repeatedly. Through repetition, which may take years and years, your body learns a new habit 'in muscle memory, not in head knowledge. You no longer must think about it; it just happens naturally. Think of an NFL quarterback: from the moment the ball is snapped to thrown, most of them do that in under three seconds. At that moment they aren't thinking about what they are doing; it is natural. Often in religious circles, people will talk about faith moving from the head to the heart, where it isn't something you 'think about' but something that comes naturally because it is a part of who you are." 1

The same can be said about our faith and the number of times we hear a spiritual truth. Eventually, it becomes second nature and a part of our everyday lives.

Big Idea: Repetition in Matters of Faith is a Good Thing and Can Lead to Joy.

In our passage today, the Apostle Paul instructs the Philippian believers to be filled with joy, especially when it comes to matters of faith. And one of the ways we can do that is by being reminded of the important truths of the Bible. In fact, he was reminding them of truths that were already taught previously.

In the reading for today in chapter 3, in verse 1 it says: "Further, my brothers and sisters, rejoice in the Lord! It is no trouble for me to write the same things to you again." First, the idea of being reminded of biblical truths is important for growth in

Philippians-Joy in Action Devotional

the Christian life. Especially when it comes to a topic of importance as joy. Our disposition often affects everything we do, so to be joyful was imperative for the church there, but also for us today by implication. However, one of the ways we can do that is by hearing things more than once.

Insight: Repetition is Also Encouraged Because It Solidifies the Foundation of Our Faith.

The apostle Paul also gives us the reasoning of repeating the truths of the bible. Because in the last part of v. 2 he tells the Philippians why, when he says: "And I do it to safeguard your faith." That means that it was to build the foundation of their faith and strengthen them. In fact, the actual word used here carries the idea of: "Firm, certain, and true." 2 Giving us the very image of solid and foundational. So, if they needed their faith to be built up, we can conclude that it is good for our faith as well.

The distinction between repeating for a purpose and just saying things again was made by Bruce Kawin, a film theorist. He said: "'repetitious and repetitive.' 'Repetitious,' says Kawin, occurs 'when a word, percept, or experience is repeated with less impact at each recurrence; repeated to no particular end, out of a lack of intention or sloppiness of thought.' On the other hand, 'repetitive happens when a word, precept or experience is repeated with equal or greater force at each occurrence.'" 3

Let us solidify our faith by repeating the truths of Scripture for growth.

Challenge: What can I call to mind and memorize to know better from the Bible? What truths can solidify the foundation of my faith today?

Pray: Thanking God for the blessing of biblical repetition as a means for growth....

Going Deeper:

The NIV Grace and Truth Study Bible when referring to this main verse shares similar ideas when it says: "Joy floods this letter. Paul rejoices whenever Christ is preached and over his anticipation of glorifying Christ through bold witness in his upcoming hearing (1:14–20). He invites his readers to share his joy as they and he suffer for Christ (2:17–18). Now he injects a summons to rejoice in the Lord, who is the constant source of joy in all circumstances (4:4,10–13). This call to joy, however, precedes a sober warning, which Paul previously delivered in person and now repeats to safeguard his friends' faith." 4

Philippians-Joy in Action Devotional

Devotion written by Pastor Frank & Samuel Gervasi

1. Illustration Ideas, https://illustrationideas.bible/muscle-memory/, as accessed on 03/02/2025.

2. Interlinear Bible,
https://www.biblestudytools.com/lexicons/greek/nas/asphales.html#google_vignette, as accessed on
03/02/2025

3. https://thepastorsworkshop.com/sermon-illustrations/william-h-willimon-the-repetitive--repetitious-
id_3483

4. NIV Grace and Truth Study Bible, Bible Gateway Plus,
https://www.biblegateway.com/passage/?search=Philippians%203%3A1-2&version=NIV, as accessed
on 03/02/2025

5. Music Intro/Outro, Praise Adonai, Integrity Music, Paul Biloche, 2009

#18 - Reliable Power
Read: *Philippians 3:3-7*

"His divine power has given us everything we need for a godly life through our knowledge of him who called us by his own glory and goodness." 2 Peter 1:3, NIV

"A young missionary, Herbert Jackson, was given a car to help him in his work. The car was a major asset, but it had one difficulty—it would not start without a push or a jump-start. Jackson devised a system to cope with the car's inability to start. When he was ready to leave his home, he went to a nearby school and asked permission to bring some of the children out of class to help him push-start his car.

Throughout the day, he was careful to always park on a hill or to leave his engine running when he stopped for short visits. For two years the young missionary used what he believed was an ingenious method to enable him to use the car.

When poor health forced the Jackson family to leave the field, a new missionary arrived to lead the mission. When Jackson explained to the new missionary his methods for starting the car, the young man opened the hood and began inspecting. 'Why, Dr. Jackson,' he interrupted, 'I believe the only trouble is the loose cable.' He gave the cable a twist, pushed the switch, and the engine roared to life.

For two years, Dr. Jackson had used his own devices and endured needless trouble. The power to start the car was there all the time—it only needed to be connected." 1

In the same way, how often do we, as children of God, try to do His will and His work by human means? As we'll see in our devotion today, while human effort is

Philippians-Joy in Action Devotional

important, it is only when we rely on the power of God that we can live the life God has called us to.

Big Idea: To live a godly life and stand on the truth, we must rely on Christ and not on human efforts.

In our passage today, the Apostle Paul makes a distinction between the "brothers and sisters" and those who willingly and systematically do evil, which he describes as dogs and "mutilators of the flesh". And when Paul describes true believers, he identifies them in an interesting way. He says in verse 3, "We rely on what Christ Jesus has done for us. We put no confidence in human effort…" (NLT)

As we've touched on in past devotions, there are disciplines in the Christian life. That means there will be times when we need to commit to doing certain things of our own volition and train ourselves to do the right thing. However, in the end, the only thing that will really make obedience last, is total reliance on Christ.

Insight: Our own efforts alone cannot produce lasting heart change, so we must lean on God for strength to obey His Word and exhibit joy.

If anyone had a right to place their confidence in their own humanity, it was Paul. Paul "was circumcised on the eighth day" and was a Pharisee. Paul kept all the rules you would look for a good Jew to keep. He was also just that – a Jew, not by converting to Judaism, but by blood. Paul could trace his ancestry back to Benjamin, one of Jacob's twelve sons in the book of Genesis.

Even in addition to his prestigious heritage and thorough compliance to the Law, Paul was also a Zealot. We know that before His conversion on the road to Damascus, He was committed to seeking any Christians he could find and persecuting them because of their faith in Christ. According to Paul's old life, he was a better Jew than most of the Judaizers in the Philippian church.

Yet what does Paul say in verse 7? "I once thought these things were valuable, but now I consider them worthless because of what Christ has done." (NLT) In the end, he realized that the only way to live a life that pleased God and brought joy to his own heart was going to be through complete trust and reliance on Christ. Likewise, our faith cannot endure if it is driven by human power. It is only when we submit to God's power and lean on His Spirit to guide us that we can live a life worth being proud of. Let's seek God for His strength to live life well today.

Challenge: In what areas do I tend to lean on my own strength? How can I teach myself to lean on God's power in this area?

Pray: Asking God to give me His power today, and to lean on Him for whatever I face...

Going Deeper:

Paul had every right by Jewish cultural standards to boast about his own accomplishments and background, and to rely on them, yet he chose dependence on Christ's merits rather than dependence on his own. In the NASB Charles F. Stanley Life Principles Bible Notes, Stanley describes it in his own words:

"Paul had astounding credentials—everything that defined success in his community. From birth, he observed the law and grew to be a very prominent Pharisee as a student of the respected Gamaliel (Acts 5:34). He could trace his lineage to the first king of Israel, Saul. Also, because he was born in Tarsus, he enjoyed all the rights and privileges of being a Roman citizen. Yet none of this could compare to knowing Christ." 2

Devotion written by Pastor Frank & Samuel Gervasi

---

1. Adapted from an illustration accessed at https://ministry127.com/resources/illustration/the-power-must-be-used, on 3/09/2025.

2. NASB Charles F. Stanley Life Principles Bible Notes, Copyright Charles F. Stanley, 2013. As accessed thru Bible Gateway Plus, at https://www.biblegateway.com/passage/?search=philippians%203%3A3-7&version=NIV, on 03/09/2025.

3. Music Intro/Outro, Praise Adonai, Integrity Music, Paul Baloche, 2009.

Philippians-Joy in Action Devotional

#19 - Relationship Value
Read: *Philippians 3:7-9*

"But whatever were gains to me I now consider loss for the sake of Christ."
Philippians 3:7, NIV

A story was about value and was said that: "One dark and stormy night, a gang of thieves broke into a jewelry store, but they were on a mission with a difference. They didn't steal anything. But they carefully went round the whole shop and switched all the price tags. Then they left. The next day, the staff came in, and because the thieves had been so careful, nobody noticed they'd even been there. Customers came and people were spending huge amounts of money to buy cheap junk, while others were paying a couple of dollars for jewelry worth thousands of dollars. Someone has switched the tags on our planet. We are continually bombarded with a different set of values from what the Bible teaches." 1

In a similar way we often place value and importance on the wrong things in life. Some will place it in education, status, money, others will place it in relationships, and a host of other things. However, our value should be in God and what was accomplished at the Cross by faith.

Big Idea: The Value of Knowing Christ Intimately Has the Greatest Value.

Philippians-Joy in Action Devotional

In our passage today, the Apostle Paul makes a powerful statement regarding his old life and the things he considered important. However, he saw them now as worthless in comparison to knowing Christ in a close, intimate way.

Starting in v. 7 he says: "I once thought these things were valuable but now, I consider them worthless because of what Christ has done." It's interesting that all the things we place as important in life can become worthless. However, that is how he was now viewing them, especially in comparison to what the Apostle Paul was considering as important, now that he was following Christ. There had been a fundamental change in everything that once was dominant in his life.

In fact, our relationship with Jesus is the MOST important relationship we can have, and one of great value. He describes his relationship with Christ as having the greatest importance. In v. 8 he says: "I consider everything a loss because of the surpassing worth of knowing Christ."

_____

Insight: The Value of Knowing Christ is Greater Even than Our Past.

_____

If anyone had a right to place their confidence in their own past, it was Paul. He was Zealous for the Law of Moses. He was trained by Gamaliel, who was a prominent Jewish Rabbi and Teacher. A Pharisee who was known as meticulous to following the Law. However, he considered his relationship with Christ even more important that his past.

Now, to the average person that may not mean a lot, because we all have different backgrounds. Nevertheless, those achievements were important in that culture and time. Whatever our past achievements they pale in comparison to our relationship with God, through Christ, in faith.

_____

Challenge: In what areas do I tend to lean on my own past achievements? How can I stand more firmly in what Christ has accomplished for me?

Pray: Asking God to give me His grace and humility to rely on fully what Christ did and not our past...

Philippians-Joy in Action Devotional

Going Deeper:

Paul had every right by Jewish cultural standards to boast about his own accomplishments and background, and to rely on them, yet he chose dependence on Christ's grace through faith rather than dependence on his own. In the Zondervan Illustrated Bible Dictionary, further explains what is often defined as Self-Righteousness when it says:

"Confidence in one's own righteousness. In popular usage, a self-righteous person is one who views himself or herself as morally upright in contrast to others; it often implies adherence to the letter of legal requirements (legalism) without regard to their spirit. In a theological sense, the term self-righteousness is applied to the belief, attitude, or behavior of persons who seek God's acceptance by their own efforts, that is, by doing good works and keeping the divine statutes. Although the term self-righteousness itself does not appear in the Bible, the concept is clearly indicated in various passages.....The self-righteous person is righteous neither in the religious nor the moral sense. Those who trust in themselves do not have right standing with God through self-effort or adherence to the law; nor are they morally upright, since only their external conduct is affected and not their attitudes. See also justification." 2

Devotion written by Pastor Frank & Samuel Gervasi

1. Hotsermon Illustrations, https://hotsermons.com/sermon-illustrations/sermon-illustrations-values.html, as accessed on 03/16/2025

2. Zondervan Illustrated Bible Dictionary, Copyright © 1987, 2011 by Zondervan, Biblegateway Plus, as accessed on 03/16/2025.

3. Music Intro/Outro, Praise Adonai, Integrity Music, Paul Baloche, 2009.

Philippians-Joy in Action Devotional

#20 - The Art of Dying
Read: *Philippians 3:8-11*

"Then he called the crowd to him along with his disciples and said: 'Whoever wants to be my disciple must deny themselves and take up their cross and follow me. For whoever wants to save their life will lose it, but whoever loses their life for me and for the gospel will save it.'"

Mark 8:34-35, NIV

A story exists of a man named James Calvert who dedicated his life to missionary work overseas. As he set out to answer God's call on his life, he had interesting interaction: "When James Calvert went as a missionary to the cannibals of the Fiji Islands, the captain of the ship sought to turn him back, crying out "You will lose your life and the lives of those with you if you go among such savages" Calvert only replied, 'We died before we came here.'" 1

When most of us hear the word "dying", we think of it as a negative thing. In most cases, funerals are no fun at all, as the family who has lost a loved one processes their grief and says their last goodbyes. However, in the Christian sense of the word, "dying" is a positive thing – particularly in relation to us dying to our old ways of life. And as we'll see as we continue our emphasis in Philippians, that kind of dying leads us to experiencing great things from God we never could otherwise.

Big Idea: Dying to self will always lead to resurrection power.

In our passage today, the Apostle Paul expresses his longing to experience the power of Christ in his own life. And Paul understands that to receive this dynamic power, there has to be a little dying. He says in verse 10, "I want to know Christ— yes, to know the power of his resurrection and participation in his sufferings, becoming like him in his death..." (NIV)

Notice the phrase "becoming like him in his death". Death is not something any of us want to go through, but without death, we could not experience resurrection power. In the garden of Gethsemane, just before His crucifixion, Jesus begged the Father to let the cup be taken from him, and to avoid the suffering He was about to endure (Matthew 26:36-46), yet in the end He chose to go to the cross and die. And because He did, we are now set free, forgiven, and promised an eternal home! In the same way, dying to our old habits and patterns of behavior can be painful, and something we prefer to avoid. But on the other hand, that discomfort is a greater blessing than we may realize.

Insight: If we are to fully experience the same power that raised Christ from the dead, we must crucify our sinful ways and desires and submit to the Holy Spirit.

Notice how verse 10 is speaking about resurrection power for the present tense, in the here and now, but verse 11 focuses on this power for the future. Verse 11 says, "...and so, somehow, attaining to the resurrection from the dead." (NIV)

One day we will actually be resurrected physically, as new creatures with fully glorified bodies in a brand-new world, free from the presence of sin and brokenness, and in the literal presence of God Himself. We can experience power and victory today, and one day will experience it in its fullness in the life to come.

If we are going to experience the mighty power of God today, we must learn to die to ourselves and live for Christ. Because nothing is more valuable than knowing Him.

Challenge: In what areas do I need to experience resurrection power today? What are some old ways I need to die to?

Pray: Asking God to give me His power today, and to help me die to my old ways...

Philippians-Joy in Action Devotional

Going Deeper:

In our passage, Paul ants to die to himself not only to experience resurrection power, but also because he wished to "know Christ" (v. 10; NIV). What did it mean for Paul to "know Christ" through dying to his old ways. In the ESV Reformation Study Bible, we can begin to see Paul's thinking behind this phrase. And understanding this truth can motivate us to seek a deeper level of closeness and intimacy with God:

"This is Paul's most passionate longing (1:20–23); he speaks not merely of greater mental awareness, but of deepened personal union. The following...clauses explain how knowing Christ is presently experienced...For Paul, identification with the crucified and risen Christ is fundamental to Christian living. Elsewhere (2 Cor. 4:7, 10, 11), Paul teaches that it is through participation in the sufferings of Christ that the power of Christ's resurrection is manifested in the life of the Christian. This identification with the sufferings of Christ is not exclusively in martyrdom (2:17) but for all of life." 2

Devotion written by Pastor Frank & Samuel Gervasi

---

1. An illustration accessed at https://sermoncentral.com/sermon-illustrations/101661/we-died-before-we-came-here-by-dr-larry-petton, on 3/23/2025.

2. ESV Reformation Study Bible, Copyright © 2008 by P&R Publishing, Biblegateway Plus, as accessed on 03/23/2025.

3. Music Intro/Outro, Praise Adonai, Integrity Music, Paul Baloche, 2009.

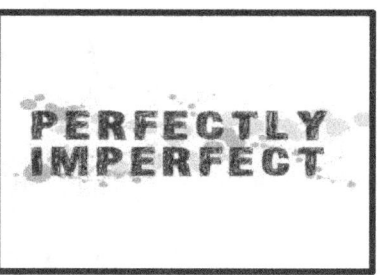

#21 - Perfectly Imperfect
Read: *Philippians 3:12-16*

"Surely there is not a righteous man on earth who does good and never sins." Ecclesiastes 7:20, ESV

I once heard a story about a small child and his father, who were sitting in church when the boy "...asked [him]...'Daddy, what is a Christian?' The dad thought for a moment, because he wanted to give a good answer to such an important question. Finally, he said, 'A Christian is a person who loves and obeys God. He loves his friends, his neighbors, and even his enemies. He is kind and gentle and prays a lot. He looks forward to going to heaven and thinks that knowing God is better than anything on this earth. That, son, is a Christian.' The little boy sat quiet for a minute, and then he said, 'Daddy, have I ever seen a Christian?'" 1

Despite what people may think, and how things may appear to those on the outside, there is no one who has arrived at the pinnacle of Christian growth. All of us are flawed and imperfect until the day we die. As we'll see in our devotion today, being honest with ourselves about where we are in our walk with Christ is what will help us grow in our faith.

Big Idea: A mature believer is realistic about his or her spiritual progress.

In previous devotions, we've seen Paul talk about things like dying to our old ways and placing no confidence in the flesh. And yet, he seems to acknowledge his own lack of completeness in both these areas in verse 12, when he says, "Not that I have already obtained all this, or have arrived at my goal..." (NIV)

What makes this confession on Paul's part so interesting, is that if we were to think about someone worthy of the title of "perfect Christian", Paul might be the first candidate for some of us. Yet, outside of Christ Jesus Himself, there is no human being currently on earth or from the pages of history who could claim such a title.

––––––––––––

Insight: None of us will ever be without flaws or failures, so we can be honest with ourselves – which will lead to the greatest spiritual growth.

––––––––––––

Understanding that we will never be perfect is a crucial step for believers. Because when we accept these natural human limitations, it helps us to live in a healthy way. Verses 15 and 16 say, "All of them, who are mature should take such a view of things. And if on some point you think differently that too God will make clear to you. Only let us live up to what we have already attained." (NIV)

Notice that it is the imperfect who are described as "mature". This word carries the idea of "brought to its end and finished".2 We cannot reach this point if we cannot accept our own imperfection.

Finally, we must understand that this verse is not saying mature Christians don't want to improve. But a mature believer understands that he will not be made fully complete until Christ steps out of heaven. He is realistic about his spiritual progress, and so he grows the most.

As we go through our day today, let's strive to hold ourselves to the proper standard and see ourselves correctly.

––––––––––––

Challenge: How do I view myself in my spiritual growth? Am I realistic about my spiritual progress?

Pray: Asking God to help me be honest with myself and grow in my walk with Him...

––––––––––––

Philippians-Joy in Action Devotional

Going Deeper:

What does it mean for believers to "take such a view of things" in verse 15? In the NKJV Evangelical Study Bible, this mindset mature believers are expected to have is expounded upon:

"Have this mind literally means 'think like this.' Those who are mature believers recognize that they are not perfect and that they have fallen short of God's expectations. Nevertheless, they tirelessly press onward in their spiritual journey, seeking to become more like Christ in each facet of their lives (see vv. 13–14). Mature believers are those who admit that they are not perfect (i.e., fully mature) but press on toward that goal." 3

Devotion written by Pastor Frank & Samuel Gervasi

---

1. An illustration accessed at https://pastorlife.com/raising-them-right/, on 4/07/2025.

2. Interlinear Bible. As accessed at https://www.biblestudytools.com/lexicons/greek/kjv/teleios.html, on 4/07/2025.

3. NKJV Evangelical Study Bible, Copyright © 2023 by Thomas Nelson. BibleGateway Plus, as accessed on 04/07/2025.

4. Music Intro/Outro, Praise Adonai, Integrity Music, Paul Baloche, 2009.

Philippians-Joy in Action Devotional

#22 – A Committed Following
Read: *Philippians 3:15-18*

"Join together in following my example." **Philippians 3:17a., NIV**

I once heard a story about "a farmer that grabbed his shotgun to shoot at a flock of pesky crows. These crows kept bothering the other wildlife on the farm. They were always eating his corn crop and a real nuisance. Unfortunately, after he shot, he didn't see his sociable pet parrot that had joined the crows. After firing a few shots, he walked over to the fallen birds and was surprised to find his badly ruffled parrot with a broken wing. To make matters worse his kids also saw. They asked, 'Dad, what happened?' The farmer simply replied, 'Bad company I guess.'" 1

Despite what people may think, we are affected by the people we are around. So, it takes wisdom to choose who we invest our time around We choose wisely because we want to grow and walk in faith.

Big Idea: We Should Live in Proper Ways-Like Christians Before Us.

In previous devotions, we've seen Paul talk about many things like dying to our old ways and placing no confidence in the flesh, and even the previous devotion which focused on a believer striving for maturity. However, he seems to paint the picture of following other Christians before us faith in verse 17, when he says, "Join together in following my example...and just as you have us model." (NIV)

Philippians-Joy in Action Devotional

Meaning, that we should conduct ourselves by living the good examples that God puts us in the path of. Now, for clarification he isn't saying that we will be around bad or less than ideal examples but that we purposely follow the lead of the effective ones.

He further reinforces that idea in the second part of verse 17 when he says: "keep your eyes on those who live as we do." (NIV). So, it shows an intentionality in observing the correct examples of people who were living correctly.

Insight: We Should Live in Proper Ways Like Those Before Us – By Being Selective Decisive, emulating their Lives.

Regardless of what we may think we are influenced by the people we spend most of our time around. We can begin to act and talk like them without even realizing it. So, it makes sense to choose and act on those good examples.

In fact, I used to hear a person say it like this: "Stick with the winners." To be honest I used to hear that and think it sounded prideful. However, I have come to see that as a wise statement that means we should be selective in who we choose to be around.

As we go through our day and week, let's strive to hold ourselves to the proper standard, see others' lives, and act correctly.

Challenge: Are we being prideful and selective for the right reasons or the wrong ones? Are we following the good examples before us? Are we acting on what we see?

Pray: Asking God to help me be honest with myself and grow in my walk with Him...

Going Deeper:

Who are the people we should follow in life? Commenting on verses 15-19 In the Grace and Truth Study Bible, show how we can live the Christian Life:

Philippians-Joy in Action Devotional

"We grow by watching and imitating good examples. Paul shows Christians how to face suffering by explaining his own reaction to chains, rivals, and the prospect of execution (1:12–26). He urges them to prefer others' needs to their own by invoking the selfless servanthood of Christ, Timothy, Epaphroditus, and himself (1:27—2:30). He protects them from legalism by narrating his own conversion from confidence in the flesh to delight in the righteousness and worth of Christ (3:2–11). Now he calls them to imitate his relentless pursuit of Christlike maturity. Paul points them to the example of those who share his mindset and his life, meaning his pattern of behavior." 2

Devotion written by Pastor Frank & Samuel Gervasi

---

1. An illustration accessed by PFG, sermon, as accessed on 4/07/2025.

2. Grace and Truth Study Bible, Copyright © 2021 by Zondervan. BibleGateway Plus, as accessed on 04/013/2025.

4. Music Intro/Outro, Praise Adonai, Integrity Music, Paul Baloche, 2009.

#23 - Citizen Living
Read: *Philippians 3:20-21*

"Therefore, we do not lose heart. Though outwardly we are wasting away, yet inwardly we are being renewed day by day. For our light and momentary troubles are achieving for us an eternal glory that far outweighs them all."

2 Corinthians 4:16-17, NIV

"In 1973, a horse named Secretariat became a legend in his time. Not only did the Secretariat win the Triple Crown of Thoroughbred Racing, but he did it with an unprecedented performance. At the Belmont Stakes, he not only won the race by 31 lengths, but he set new records along the way as he went faster with each phase of the run. For one-and-one-half miles, that famous thoroughbred ran faster every second. Secretariat was accelerating at such an incredible pace that his trainer noted if the race had been extended to another lap, his heart would have literally exploded. It is always tempting to settle into status quo performance, but the greatest joy is found in straining ahead to not just finish, but to finish well..." [1]

In the same way the Secretariat gained momentum as the longer he ran, we should keep pressing on until the end. And as we'll see in Philippians today, our eternal destination should give us the hope and encouragement we need to finish with strength and courage.

Big Idea: We should press forward with diligence to the prize we have waiting in our eternal home.

Philippians-Joy in Action Devotional

In previous devotions, we've talked extensively about living different from the world, relying on the power of God, and following in the obedient footsteps of those before us. But doing these things can be tiring and exhausting, and it's easy to lose steam the longer we press on in life. However, in verse 20, Paul directs our attention to a driving and motivating truth that should carry us – the promise of heaven: "But our citizenship is in heaven. And we eagerly await a Savior from there, the Lord Jesus Christ…" (NIV)

Our citizenship is highlighted in stark contrast to the earlier verses, which describe the enemies of the cross – those whose minds are "set on earthly things" (v. 19). The Christian turns his mind away from these things, because of the hope he received from the promise of heaven.

Insight: Regardless of the length of time involved, we should persevere in godliness and wait expectantly for our coming reward.

Concerning this promise for the future, the Apostle Paul even gives us the how and why. The why is easier: because that future is all contingent on God. Verse 21 says, "…who, by the power that enables him to bring everything under his control, will transform our lowly bodies so that they will be like his glorious body." (NIV)

However, the how does require something more out of us. It requires a good and proper focus! Which overtime can be difficult to maintain, especially over hard and difficult seasons. But if our eyes are set on the promise instead of the problem, we will find strength to keep on keeping on.

Charles Stanley says it like this: "When we die, we will immediately be in the presence of Almighty God. As believers, we will no longer remember the struggles and sorrows of this life because our minds and bodies will be absolutely purified in His presence…everything will be different, because we will stand holy and glorified before the Lord." 2

Let's choose to set our minds on this promise today, and to wait eagerly for the fulfillment of that promise. Because if that promise is true, then we can run on confident and empowered to finish the race.

Philippians-Joy in Action Devotional

Challenge: Am I pressing forward with everything I must win the prize, or has my pace grown slower? How can I meditate on this promise throughout my day?

Pray: Asking God to help us persevere in our faith, remembering the promises He gave and the wonderful place He's prepared...

Going Deeper:

The church at Philippi was well acquainted with the concept of citizenship – the residents of Philippi inherited Roman citizenship from birth, were granted special privileges from the state. Perhaps that is why Paul referred to them as "citizens of heaven" (v. 20). The NIV Biblical Theology Study Bible says this regarding Philippians 3:20:

"There is an explicit contrast here between 'us,' Christians whose citizenship is in heaven, and those whose minds are 'set on earthly things' (v. 19). There is also an implied contrast with the Roman citizenship that the Philippians enjoyed: they were grafted into an ancient Roman family line that is celebrated in several first-century inscriptions from the city, and they received a number of taxation privileges. As a mere earthly matter, they cannot put their confidence in Roman citizenship (cf. v. 3; see Acts 16:37), since they are citizens of heaven. we eagerly await. Christians anticipate Christ's return and the bodily resurrection (Rom 8:23)." 3

Devotion written by Pastor Frank & Samuel Gervasi

---

1. An illustration accessed at https://ministry127.com/resources/illustration/finish-well, on 4/20/2025.

2. Quote by Charles F. Stanley, NASB, The Charles F. Stanley Life Principles Bible: Holy Bible, New American Standard Bible, as accessed at https://www.goodreads.com/author/quotes/39628.Charles_F_Stanley#:~:text=When%20we%20die%2C%20we%20will,absolutely%20purified%20in%20His%20presence., on 4/20/2025.

2. NIV Biblical Theology Study Bible, Copyright © 2019 by Zondervan. BibleGateway Plus, as accessed on 04/20/2025.

4. Music Intro/Outro, Praise Adonai, Integrity Music, Paul Baloche, 2009.

Philippians-Joy in Action Devotional

#24 - Grounded Joy
Read: *Philippians 4:4-7*

"Join together in following my example." **Philippians 3:17a., NIV**

I once heard a story about "a farmer that grabbed his shotgun to shoot at a flock of pesky crows. These crows kept bothering the other wildlife on the farm. They were always eating his corn crop and a real nuisance. Unfortunately, after he shot, he didn't see his sociable pet parrot that had joined the crows. After firing a few shots, he walked over to the fallen birds and was surprised to find his badly ruffled parrot with a broken wing. To make matters worse his kids also saw. They asked, 'Dad, what happened?' The farmer simply replied, 'Bad company I guess.'" 1

Despite what people may think, we are affected by the people we are around. So, it takes wisdom to choose who we invest our time around We choose wisely because we want to grow and walk in faith.

Big Idea: Joy Should Be Rooted and Grounded in Christ.

In today's devotion the Apostle expands on the concept of joy by showing us some of the reasons a person can be joyful. However, he seems to paint the picture of where our joy is rooted and grounded. If we look in verse 4, he says, "Rejoice in the Lord always. I will say it again: Rejoice!" (NIV)

There are a couple of important things to be noticed in that verse. First, joy is grounded in Christ. The statement, "In the Lord." is making that distinction.

Secondly, however, notice that it was a command given in an imperative mood. Some of the earliest translations and manuscripts didn't include punctuation. However, when committees met together to make some newer translations easier to read, it was added. That's why some translators put an exclamation point. Which was important because joy is very critical to life. Additionally, another thing to point out is that he was reiterating that believers "should rejoice."

———————————

Insight: Joy Should Be Rooted and Grounded in Christ Because Otherwise It Won't Last...

———————————

Our culture often confuses Joy with happiness. Consequently, we are also influenced by this common mindset if we are not careful. Joy is lasting, stable, and grounded because it is not placed in superficial circumstances. In fact, Joy is not dependent on circumstances at all.

See, happiness is because of things like we got a raise at work. However, it turns sadness when we realize the company has more demands of us. Happiness is payday is here but gone as the money runs out. Joy is, "And my God will meet all your needs according to the riches of his glory in Christ Jesus." Philippians 4:19, NIV.)

Joy will always outlast circumstantial happiness. Because Joy is rooted and placed in God and His abilities to provide everything, we need in life.

Charles Spurgeon said this about joy: "I do not think the church rejoices enough. We all grumble enough and groan enough: but very few of us rejoice enough." 2

Let us be known for rejoicing in Christ and thank God for His Love and provision today in life today.

———————————

Challenge: Are we rooting and grounding our joy in Christ or are we trying somewhere else? What is our mindset? Do I base my disposition in circumstances or God?

Pray: Asking God to help me be Joyful in all things because of our faith in Him...

_____

Going Deeper:

Commenting on verses 4-6, the NIV Grace and Truth Study Bible, expands the difference between Happiness and joy when it says:

"Paul begins to close the letter with a series of directions, commending joy (again), gentleness, prayer, and a focus on what is good and beautiful, and promising God's peace and presence. Again, he locates the source of constant joy as the Lord, not circumstances, which fluctuate widely (vv. 11–13; Hab 3:17–18)." 2

_____

Devotion written by Pastor Frank & Samuel Gervasi

_____

1. Spurgeon Quotes, https://www.spurgeon.org/resource-library/blog-entries/12-spurgeon-quotes-on-joy/, as accessed on 4/27/2025.

2. NIV Grace and Truth Study Bible, Copyright © 2021 by Zondervan. BibleGateway Plus, as accessed on 04/027/2025.

3. Music Intro/Outro, Praise Adonai, Integrity Music, Paul Baloche, 2009.

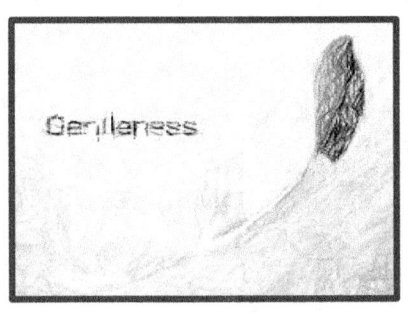

#25 - A Gentle Witness
Read: *Philippians 4:4-5*

"Be completely humble and gentle; be patient, bearing with one another in love." **Ephesians 4:2, NIV**

I once heard a story about a man who bought a fish tank for his children, and a series of unfortunate events that followed: "At their school carnival, our kids won four free goldfish...so out I went Saturday morning to find an aquarium. The first few I priced ranged from $40 to $70. Then I spotted it--right in the aisle: a discarded 10-gallon display tank, complete with gravel and filter--for a mere five bucks. Sold! Of course, it was nasty dirty, but the savings made the two hours of clean-up a breeze. Those four new fish looked great in their new home, at least for the first day. But by Sunday one had died...Monday morning revealed a second casualty, and by Monday night a third goldfish had gone belly up. We called in an expert, a member of our church who [had] a 30-gallon tank. It didn't take him long to discover the problem: I had washed the tank with soap, an absolute no-no." The harshness of the residue the soap left behind had killed the inhabitants of the aquarium. "My uninformed efforts had destroyed the very lives I was trying to protect." 1

A lack of gentleness can be harmful to those around us, like the soap was to the goldfish. But on the other hand, a life characterized by an abundance of gentleness can say more about the impact Jesus has on us than our words ever could. As we'll see in our devotion today, the joy we receive from knowing and following Jesus should be the catalyst that drives us to pursue a gentle heart.

Big Idea: A life of gentleness shows others the joy we have in Christ.

In our passage today, the Apostle Paul relates relentless rejoicing in the Lord with this attitude of gentleness, saying in verse 5: "Let your gentleness be evident to all; the Lord is near." (NIV)

Some versions replace the word "gentleness" with "a gentle spirit" (NASB), "moderation" (KJV), or "Let others see that you are considerate…" (NLT) The original word carries all these ideas with it. It means "suitable, equitable, mild, fair, and gentle". 2

What do all these words and definitions have to do with joy? The point is this: a joyous person that's filled with excitement and gratitude, will likely embody that joyfulness through a gentle spirit in their interactions with others. One who is walking in the Spirit and experiencing true joy exemplifies it through gentle living.

Insight: Joy can be seen by others in how we live, so let's strive to embody a gentle heart.

Consider the fact that it would be difficult for a person to be filled with the kind of excitement and gladness we've discussed throughout the entirety of Philippians without showing it. Joy is an emotion that's expressive and should appear outwardly to those around us.

Finally, notice the second part of the verse, which gives one more reason why a Christian ought to be thankful. Verse 5 says, "The Lord is near." (NIV)

The fact that Jesus is coming back both physically and visibly, and is coming soon, should fill us with such joy and thankfulness, it overflows into how we interact with others! Let's choose to embody gentleness today, to show a watching world the joy we have from being called children of God.

Challenge: In what areas do I need to embody gentleness today? How can I show others the joy that God gives me?

Philippians-Joy in Action Devotional

Pray: Asking God to help me pursue a gentle spirit today...

Going Deeper:

What does it mean that "the Lord is near"? In the NIV Case for Christ Study Bible, Lee Strobel says this regarding the return of Jesus:

"The next great event in God's prophetic schedule is Christ's return. The whole period from Christ's first coming to the consummation of the kingdom is viewed in the NT as the last time (see 1Jn 2:18 and note). From God's vantage point, 'a thousand years are like a day' (2Pe 3:8; see note there). Thus, there is a sense in which, for every generation, the Lord's coming is near." 3

Devotion written by Pastor Frank & Samuel Gervasi

---

1. An illustration accessed at https://www.sermonillustrations.com/a-z/g/gentleness.htm, on 5/4/2025.

2. Epieikes, Interlinear Bible. https://www.biblestudytools.com/lexicons/greek/nas/epieikes.html, as accessed on 5/05/2025.

3. NIV Case for Christ Study Bible, Copyright © 2009 by Lee Strobel. All rights reserved. BibleGateway Plus, as accessed on 5/05/2025.

4. Music Intro/Outro, Praise Adonai, Integrity Music, Paul Baloche, 2009.

Philippians-Joy in Action Devotional

#26 - Joy in Practice
Read: *Philippians 4:6-7*

"The poor will eat and be satisfied. All who seek the Lord will praise him. Their hearts will rejoice with everlasting joy." **Psalm 22:26, NLT**

I once heard a story about George Mueller, and it was said that he gratefully relied on prayer. The story goes: "One of main works of his life was the establishment of a large orphanage at Bristol, England. In 64 years from the outset of this work, Mr. Mueller cared for 10,024 orphans, established 7-day schools which 81,501 children attended; founded 12 Sunday schools which instructed a total of 32,944 children: and aided 25 Sunday schools in England and Wales. He contributed large sums of money to foreign mission work, distributed 1,989,266 Bibles and parts thereof, circulated 3,101,338 books and tracts, and traveled in 42 countries preaching the Gospel to 3,000,000 hearers. In all, he received from and gave back to God $7,500,000; at no time asking anyone for so much as a penny.

He was a man who knew by experience what it is for God to 'give us this day our daily bread.' He remarked, 'From August 1838, to April, 1849, we had day by day, almost without interruption, to look to Him for our daily supplies, and, for a great part of the time, from meal to meal.' Materials were not the only things this man of God received in answered prayer. He made this statement: 'Thousands of souls have been saved in answer to my prayers.'" 1

Joy is put into action by prayer. So, it makes sense to pray about everything, all the time. For the Christian the actual feet to our faith is seen in one way by how much we pray.

Big Idea: Joy is Put into Practice—By A Person's Prayer Life.

───────────────

As we move along to the final stretch of the devotion's emphasis in Philippians, we see Joy in Action. Specifically, through how and when a person prays. Meaning that a joyful person has developed the habit of when something comes up, they bring it before God by talking with Him about it. Not hanging on to it and then thinking and festering about it but immediately finds themselves before the Throne.

Look at v. 5, "Do not be anxious about anything, but in every situation, by prayer and petition, with thanksgiving, present your requests to God." NIV

Considering this, even joyful people have setbacks in life, don't they? They're not immune to problems basically. However, the difference may be in the response. Because one person goes into dwelling and festering but the other goes to God and leaves it in His hands.

Conversely, the unjoyful person allows the circumstances to affect their attitude in a negative way. But the joyful person gives it to God and goes back to being positive about life. The unjoyful person allows anxiety to take over and control their thoughts, but the joyful person learns to bring every request and petition to God.

───────────────

Insight: A Joyful Person's Prayer Life Will Be Extensive and Full of Various Prayers with Gratitude

───────────────

Meaning, that it is not only put into practice by regular prayer by shown by the different types of prayers being offered up to God. If we look at the second part of verse 5, the Apostle shows a couple of ways. Because "By prayer" NIV implies the longer, regular, more structured requests like we may put on a prayer list to keep us focused.

However, "Petitions" give an image of the daily things that come to mind throughout the day by the Holy Spirit. An example might be we see a person and we get a thought because they remind us of someone we know. So, we use that as an opportunity to pray for that person quickly as we are going along.

Finally, the other ingredient the Apostle Paul gives us for putting prayer into practice is the phrase, "with Thanksgiving." The joyful individual understands the importance of a thankful attitude. So, he or she makes sure we approach God with gratitude when we pray.

See, one is trusting in themselves and their abilities but the other in rooted in faith in God's abilities.

David Jeremiah says it like this: "No matter what our circumstances, we can find a reason to be thankful." 2 With God at the forefront of our minds and life we can rejoice and be grateful for so many things.

_____

Challenge: Are we practicing our joy through prayer or not? What is our prayer life like? Do I base my requests and petitions on circumstances or God's goodness?

Pray: Asking God to help us put Joy into action through prayer, regardless of our individual circumstances...

_____

Going Deeper:

Commenting, the NIV Grace and Truth Study Bible, expands the reasons the Philippians, and us, could pray with gratitude when it says:

"Paul supports his exhortations to thankful prayer and thinking on godly things with promises of protection from anxiety by the peace of God (v. 7) and the presence of the God of peace (v. 9). The Philippians' suffering at the hands of local opponents, whatever form it took, as well as their concerns over the woes of Paul and Epaphroditus, gave them reason to worry. But, as Jesus assures us, such troubles are never outside the control of the sovereign God, who is our loving Father (Mt 6:25–34). The antidote to anxiety is prayer, presenting to God our requests regarding every sort of concern while genuinely thanking him for his constant, generous provision (Col 3:15–17).3

_____

Devotion written by Pastor Frank & Samuel Gervasi

---

1. Ministry 127, https://ministry127.com/resources/illustration/the-joy-of-the-lord-is-better-than-the-pleasures-of-sin, as accessed on 04/28/2025.

2. 30 favorite Christian Quotes on Thankfulness, https://www.crosswalk.com/faith/spiritual-life/30-christian-quotes-about-thankfulness.html , as accessed on 5/10/2025.

3. NIV Grace and Truth Study Bible, Copyright © 2021 by Zondervan. BibleGateway Plus, as accessed on 05/010/2025.

4. Music Intro/Outro, Praise Adonai, Integrity Music, Paul Baloche, 2009.

#27 - Transcendent Peace
Read: *Philippians 4:6-7*

"And let the peace of Christ rule in your hearts, to which indeed you were called in one body. And be thankful." **Colossians 3:15, ESV**

"During the French war, a train carrying dispatches to the headquarters was compelled to go over sixty miles of very rough track and reach its destination within an hour. The engineer was the bearer of the dispatches, and his wife and child were in the coach. Every moment threatened to pitch the train over the embankment or over a bridge, and, as it rolled from side to side, leaping at times almost in the air, rushing past stations, the few people inside held their breath and often cried out with terror as they sped along. There was one on that train who knew nothing of their fears and that was the child of the engineer. Happy as a bird, she laughed aloud when asked if she were not afraid, and looked up and answered, 'Why, my father is at the engine.'" 1

Peace can be an elusive thing, but those of us who place our full confidence in God and take joy in Him will find that peace naturally follows. As we'll see in our devotion today, peace is available to us because of our relationship with Christ.

Big Idea: Joy in the Lord and faithful prayer will always bring peace, because we've invested our time wisely.

Philippians-Joy in Action Devotional

In our previous passage, we examined the importance of putting in the time to pray, and how doing so leads to joy in us. In today's passage, we see how this intimate prayer life also gives us peace, as we see in verse 7: "And the peace of God, which transcends all understanding, will guard your hearts and your minds in Christ Jesus." (NIV)

A Christian who takes joy in their walk with God will experience peace. Nevertheless, we must place it there, shouldn't we? We need to commit to not only take our requests before God, but leave them at the foot of His throne, if we are to experience this transcendent Peace the passage speaks of.

Insight: Peace will be a direct result of learning and developing the habit of disciplined prayer.

Furthermore, it's also important to acknowledge that the peace of God is different than the way we may think of peace. The peace of God is not the absence of conflict or discouragement, but an attitude of trust and courage given by God to face those difficulties. God's peace is tranquil and harmonious, exempt from the rage and chaos occurring around us.

One writer says it like this: "True...peace is not found in positive thinking, in absence of conflict, or in good feelings. It comes from knowing God is in control. Our citizenship in Christ's kingdom is sure, our destiny is set, and we can have victory over sin. Let God's peace guards your heart against anxiety." 2

What a radically different type of peace! This peace is something we all need, and it causes joyfulness. Taking joy in the God we know and pouring out our hearts in prayer before Him will produce transcendent peace. Let's strive to take hold of it today!

Challenge: How does taking joy in God lead to peace? What things do I need to bring before God in prayer?

Pray: Asking God to give me His peace for the challenges I face ahead...

Philippians-Joy in Action Devotional

Going Deeper:

What exactly does the "peace of God" mean? The NRSV Cultural Backgrounds Study Bible examines the original word and its connotations, and says the following:

"Philosophers could speak of peace as tranquility in contrast with anxiety (cf. v. 6), but peace could also carry its more common sense of harmony with one another (cf. v. 2; see note on 2.1–4). guard your hearts. If "guard" carries any of its frequent military sense, it reinforces by means of irony the latter sense of peace. Prayers for peace (e.g., Num 6.26; Ps 122.8) covered one's full well-being." 3

Devotion written by Pastor Frank & Samuel Gervasi

1. An illustration accessed at https://ministry127.com/resources/illustration/her-father-was-at-the-engine, on 5/19/2025.

2. Author Unknown. Quote accessed at https://www.gracechurchwaycross.com/post/sermon-for-third-sunday-in-easter-2021, on 5/19/2025.

3. NRSV Cultural Backgrounds Study Bible, Copyright © 2019 by Zondervan. BibleGateway Plus, as accessed on 05/19/2025.

4. Music Intro/Outro, Praise Adonai, Integrity Music, Paul Baloche, 2009.

#28 - Joy Maintenance
Read: *Philippians 4:8*

"You make known to me the path of life; you will fill me with joy in your presence, with eternal pleasures at your right hand." **Psalm 16:11, NIV**

Joy is critical when it comes to life and has always been an important topic for writers over the years. In fact, it was noted by Psychology Today in 2009 that the books written on the subject jumped significantly. They were noted as saying that: "Books Published on Happiness in 2008, 4,000 books, were published on happiness which is significantly more than the 50 which were published in 2000. If people would read the Bible, they would find the key to true joy." 1 That would be a 7900% increase in book sales on the subject.

Confirming what many Christians already know about the topic. And Joy is kept strong and vibrant by the things we dwell on. So, it makes sense to think about productive things that can help us in the long run.

Big Idea: Joy is Maintained by the Things We Think About.

As we move along to the last few reflections in Philippians, we see Joy being solidifying for the long haul. Specifically, through how and what we spend our time thinking about. Meaning that a joyful person has developed the habit of doing what is necessary to maintain it. Mostly because by this point we've realized that Joy is productive and beneficial. So, we try to do whatever it takes to maintain it because of its value.

Look at v. 8, "Finally, brothers and sisters,....—if anything is excellent or praiseworthy—think about such things.." NIV

Considering this, we spend more time thinking about so many things throughout our day. However, we never really think about how our thoughts can impact our disposition. So, to be productive and efficient in keeping our joy, we should be deliberate in the things we invest our thoughts in. Dwelling might be a better word for our purposes in this reflection. Because it's probably not the quick thoughts that might come to us, but the ones we invest time and dwell on.

Insight: A Person's Joy Will Be Maintained Not only by What Think About-But Also by What Don't Think About as Well.

See, equally is important what we intentionally avoid spending our time thinking about. Because there are always things that will be better to avoid all together. Looking at the entire v. 8 the Apostle Paul lists several different things when he says: "whatever is true, whatever is noble, whatever is right, whatever is pure, whatever is lovely, whatever is admirable." NIV.

I always thought this was a blanket statement about our thoughts. However, he is really speaking about various things. "True" carries this idea of a high level of integrity. "Noble" is speaking about "Things worth reverencing." The word "right" is the same word used for "righteousness." "Pure" is referring to "of being pure from carnality and fault." Lastly, "lovely" is speaking about "acceptable and pleasing." 2

Tony Evans says it like this: "One of the reasons we don't keep our peace is that we tend to dwell on the things that are set in opposition to the peace we're asking for. If we continue to entertain messages that work against our peace, anxiety will soon return."3 With God's things at the forefront of our minds and life we can rejoice and maintain our joy for anything that life throws at us.

Challenge: Are we seeking to maintain our joy through thoughts or not? What do we spend our time thinking about? What mostly occupies our minds?

Philippians-Joy in Action Devotional

Pray: *Asking God to help us keep Joy into action through our thought life.*

Going Deeper:

Commenting, the NIV Application Bible Original Meaning Notes, expands the list of virtues when it says:

"The list of virtues that Paul asks the Philippians to "think about" could have been embraced by many right-thinking people in ancient times. This list reminds the Philippians that although society sometimes seems hostile and evil, it is still part of God's world and contains much good. 4

Devotion written by Pastor Frank & Samuel Gervasi

---

1. Ministry127, https://ministry127.com/resources/illustrations/joy, as accessed on 05/24/2025.

2. Maintaining Joy Sermon, PFG Philippians Series #9, www.MidwestChristianPublishing.com, as accessed on 05/24/ 2025.

3. CSB Tony Evans Study Bible, Copyright © 2017 by Holman Bible Publishers.. BibleGateway Plus, as accessed on 05/24/2025.

4. NIV Application Bible Original Meaning Notes, Application Notes, copyright © 2025, BibleGatewayPlus.com, as accessed on 05/24/2025

5. Music Intro/Outro, Praise Adonai, Integrity Music, Paul Baloche, 2009.

Philippians-Joy in Action Devotional

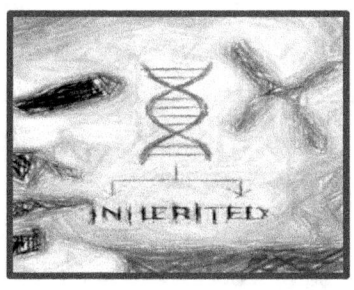

#29 - An Inherited Example
Read: *Philippians 4:8-9*

_____

"Therefore, since we are surrounded by such a great cloud of witnesses, let us throw off everything that hinders and the sin that so easily entangles. And let us run with perseverance the race marked out for us." **Hebrews 12:1, NIV**

_____

According to genetics, each person has certain genes passed down to them from their parents. Some of those characteristics that are passed down come only through the father, or only through the mother. For example, one writer notes how a child's height, gender, and fat storage are all primarily influenced by the father's chromosomes. This writer says, "When we think of inheritance, our minds often jump to the physical traits passed down from parents to their offspring. However, genetics play a fascinating role in determining much more than just eye color or height. In the captivating realm of inheritance, fathers contribute...various aspects of their children's lives, from personality quirks to innate talents." 1

When we say that a person inherits something, we are saying they had something passed down to them from someone who went before them, such as money or possessions left behind by a loved one, or, genes passed down to us by our parents!

In the same way, we have been left an inspiring and upright example by those believers who have gone before us, of how to live in a way that honors God. And, as we near the end of our journey through Philippians, we will see the importance of following that example and applying it to daily living.

_____

Big Idea: Joy is maintained by following the sound example seen in others and applying it to real-life situations.

In our passage today, the Apostle Paul encourages his readers to mimic the spiritual habits and practices they have seen from him. Verse 8 says, "Whatever you have learned, or received, or heard from me, or seen in me, put it into practice." (NIV)

What was Paul known for? Before his conversion, he was known as a strict Pharisee and persecutor of the church. But after coming to Christ, Paul was known for passionately and systematically bringing the Gospel to the Gentiles. He fought to influence the early church to accept that faith was through Christ alone, and law-keeping was no longer necessary to please God. Paul was all about serving, and living his life for God, with joy maintained consistently through everything. It is this example Paul passed down, and he wanted the Philippians to follow it.

Insight: If we want to experience joy over the long haul, in the different circumstances of life, we need to live in sound ways taught and demonstrated by those who went before us.

Furthermore, look back at the last part of verse 8: "...put it into practice." While we have been given a great example, it isn't useful until we put it into practice! Only knowing the right thing to do will not maintain joy; we must apply it. Just like we read in James 1:22-24: "But don't just listen to God's word. You must do what it says. Otherwise, you are only fooling yourselves. For if you listen to the word and don't obey, it is like glancing at your face in a mirror. You see yourself, walk away, and forget what you look like." (NLT)

We have a sound example that has been passed down to us on how to maintain joy through holy living. It is our responsibility to follow that example and carry it out. And if we do just that, our joy can withstand the test of time, through the ups and downs of this world.

Philippians-Joy in Action Devotional

Challenge: *Who is a believer in my life who has left me a sound example? In what areas do I need to follow that example to maintain joy?*

Pray: *Thanking God for the example I've inherited, and asking Him to help me live up to that standard...*

Going Deeper:

What was it about Paul that made such a good example for the Philippians to look up to? The NIV Quest Study Bible explains it like this:

"The Philippians were to handle things the way they had seen Paul handle things. He was in prison, but he was praising God instead of worrying. One of the purposes of the church is to connect believers with other kingdom-minded people. We need support, and we need good examples. When we're rejoicing and praying and dwelling on the right things and watching the right people, we don't just have the peace of God, we have the God of peace. We get his peace, and we get his presence." 2

Devotion written by Pastor Frank & Samuel Gervasi

---

1. Adapted from a story accessed on https://www.familyeducation.com/family-life/relationships/history-genealogy/6-traits-babies-inherit-from-their-father, on 6/02/2025.

2. NIV Quest Study Bible, Copyright © 1994, 2003, 2011 by Zondervan. BibleGateway Plus, as accessed on 06/02/2025.

3. Music Intro/Outro, Praise Adonai, Integrity Music, Paul Baloche, 2009.

#30 - Joy's Benefits
Read: *Philippians 4:9-13*

"Praise the Lord, my soul, and forget not all his benefits." **Psalm 103:2, NIV**

It's said that: "Thousands of people each year visit the Winchester Mansion in San Jose, California. This massive structure was built by Sarah Winchester, the widow of the gun company owner. For thirty-eight years, from 1884 until her death in 1922, the house was under constant construction. Teams of carpenters, masons and other workers were employed around the clock. Various stories have been told about the reason for this unusual practice. Most center on Mrs. Winchester's belief that she either was haunted or would be haunted by the ghosts of those killed by her husband's weapons unless she kept building her house. Others claim that she thought she would not die as long as the building continued.

Whatever the reason, she continued ordering more renovations and construction as long as she lived. There are more than 10,000 windows in the Winchester Mansion, doorways and stairs that lead to blank walls, and some 160 rooms in total. It is estimated that she spent more than $70,000,000 in today's money on largely pointless construction—all in a desperate search for peace that was ultimately doomed to fail." [1]

Many people look for peace in outward circumstances and things, just like Sarah Winchester might have. However, Christ is where peace comes from as we have discovered and realized looking at the book of Philippians these past thirty devotions.

Big Idea: Joy Maintenance is Contingent on Living in the Benefit of Peace.

———————

As we close out our devotions in Philippians, we see Joy being finalized and applied. Specifically, through what we focus our time applying and putting onto practice is what will make a difference in the end. Meaning that a joyful person has learned and developed the regular habit of spending time in God's presence. Mostly because we see the benefits it has in our life. So, we try to do whatever it takes to have that regular time in God's presence.

Look at v. 9, "And the God of peace—will be with you." NIV

Considering this, not only is God's peace that transcends understanding available, because we've prayed. It also accompanies the person who is walking in His presence, because we are putting it into practice. It seems that it's that cause-in-effect relationship between those who put into practice everything that had been learned, received, heard, or seen.

———————

Insight: The Greatest Benefit is the Peace That's Needed for Life's Ups & Downs.

———————

See, equally important is what the actual benefits are to maintaining this joy that was present in the Apostle Paul amid his circumstances. You may remember that the definition for peace was "A state of national peace and tranquility exempt from the rages and havoc of war." So, God's peace is that silent, tranquil, calmness even when everything around us is crazy. That is a real benefit when seeking to be joyful, isn't it?

Matthew Henry said: "peace is such a precious jewel that I would give anything for it...."2 Amen to that vital truth. Let us strive for the peace that can come only through Christ and living in His presence.

———————

Challenge: Are we seeking to maintain our joy through Christ's presence? How much time do we spend in His presence?

Pray: Asking God to help us maintain regular time walking in His presence.

Philippians-Joy in Action Devotional

Going Deeper:

Commenting, the NIV Grace and Truth Study Bible, explains it's view of peace when it says:

"4:6–9 Paul supports his exhortations to thankful prayer and thinking on godly things with promises of protection from anxiety by the peace of God (v. 7) and the presence of the God of peace (v. 9). The Philippians' suffering at the hands of local opponents, whatever form it took, as well as their concerns over the woes of Paul and Epaphroditus, gave them reason to worry. But, as Jesus assures us, such troubles are never outside the control of the sovereign God, who is our loving Father (Mt 6:25–34). The antidote to anxiety is prayer, presenting to God our requests regarding every sort of concern while genuinely thanking him for his constant, generous provision (Col 3:15–17). Rehearsing God's lavish grace and expressing our confident dependence on him are means by which his peace— peace that finds no explanation in our circumstances—surrounds our fragile hearts and minds in divine protective custody. The God of peace also assures us of his presence as we focus our thoughts on virtues that reflect his beautiful holiness." 3

Devotion written by Pastor Frank & Samuel Gervasi

---

1. Ministry127, https://ministry127.com/resources/illustration/peace-comes-from-following-christ, as accessed on 06/08, 2025.

2. Christian Quotes of the Day, https://christianquote.com/category/peace, as accessed on 06/08/2025.

3. NIV Grace and Truth Study Bible, https://christianquote.com/category/peace, as accessed on 06/08/2025.

5. Music Intro/Outro, Praise Adonai, Integrity Music, Paul Baloche, 2009.

Philippians-Joy in Action Devotional

www.ingramcontent.com/pod-product-compliance
Lightning Source LLC
Chambersburg PA
CBHW071319130626
46556CB00004B/1660